PRACTICING PRESENCE

PRACTICING PRESENCE

The Spirituality of Caring in Everyday Life

KERRY WALTERS

Franklin, Wisconsin

As an apostolate of the Priests of the Sacred Heart, a Catholic religious congregation, the mission of Sheed & Ward is to publish books of contemporary impact and enduring merit in Catholic Christian thought and action. The books published, however, reflect the opinion of their authors and are not meant to represent the official position of the Priests of the Sacred Heart.

2001

Sheed & Ward
7373 South Lovers Lane Road
Franklin, Wisconsin 53132
1-800-266-5564

Printed in the United States of America

Cover and interior design: Madonna Gauding
Cover art used with permission from PhotoDisc 2000.

Library of Congress Cataloging-in-Publication Data

Walters, Kerry S.
   Practicing presence: the spirituality of caring in everyday life / Kerry Walters.
      p. cm.
      ISBN 1-58051-098-1 (alk. paper)
      1. Caring—Religious aspects—Christianity. I. Title.

BV4647.S9 W35 2001
241'.677—dc21

                                                          00-067035

1 2 3 4 5 / 04 03 02 01

For Jessica Powers,
who knew how to care

Come to expand our hearts
with the calm, smooth flow of your bounty, O Lord.
Now smoothly stretch out the hide of my heart,
Grown old and shrivelled in an idle breast.
Unfold its wrinkles,
draw out its hiding place,
enlarge its vessels,
that without measure
I may yearn for you,
without measure contain you,
and that your holy capacity
may give me greater capacity.

—Gilbert of Hoyland (twelfth century)

Contents

Introduction

Becoming Saints

The glory of God is a human being living fully.

—St. Irenaeus

Uncommon Humans

The novelist Graham Greene once remarked that the proper goal of all Christians is sainthood.[1] This is a troublesome observation for many of us, usually because we're confused about what it means to be a saint.

For some, the word dredges up associations that leave us feeling awkward, even uncomfortable. It reminds us of the hagiographic tales and garish prayer cards of childhood, religious kitsch so piously saccharine that the unintended effect was off-putting rather than inspirational. For others, it suggests an other-worldly perfection that's simply too daunting. We see a saint as someone who lives a harshly ascetic existence, sternly repressing his or her "fallen" humanity to vault toward an angelic existence utterly beyond reproach. We may marvel at such fantastic creatures, but draw the line at following their path. Give up everything that makes life worthwhile—good company, sunshine, erotic love, worldly success—for a bleak monastic cell? No thank you! One day, perhaps, when old age has dried up the river of passion that surges through us; but not now. As the young Augustine famously prayed, "Lord, make me chaste—but not just yet!"[2]

In either case, sainthood evokes images that threaten

our ideas of the good life: an almost cartoonish sanctimony on the one hand, joy-repudiating withdrawal on the other. Of course, these two ways of thinking about sainthood are caricatures. But like all caricatures, they gesture at truth. Sainthood *does* involve an aura of sanctity distasteful to those of us soured by unimaginative catechism lessons, but genuine sanctity has nothing to do with plaster-cast unctuousness. Sainthood *does* demand everything of us, but instead of requiring that we dourly forsake the pleasures of life, it invites us to transfigure them into the joyful celebrations they're meant to be.

In short, genuine sainthood both liberates us from syrupy piety and allows us to live more abundantly than we ever dreamed possible. It's our destiny, our natural condition, that for which we were created. The sanctity of sainthood, if we but knew it, completes rather than retards our humanity. As Thomas Merton wrote, sainthood "is not a matter of being *less* human, but *more* human." It's a state of heightened sensitivity that increases our capacity "for concern, for suffering, for understanding, for sympathy, [but] also for humor, for joy, for appreciation of the good and beautiful things of life."[3] Merton put the point even more succinctly elsewhere. Far from saintliness and humanness being at odds with each other, "we cannot be saints unless we are first of all human."[4] Becoming a saint, then, means becoming a human.

At first glance, Merton's claim is puzzling. After all, we *are* humans, aren't we? What sense does it make, then, to talk about becoming what we already are? The confusion disappears once we realize that the word *human* can be used in either a descriptive or prescriptive way. In its first sense, it simply refers to membership in a biological class: any organism that belongs to *homo sapiens* is properly designated "human." But in the second sense, the evaluative or prescriptive one, "human" connotes a perfecting of those qualities essential to *full* humanhood. We are born humans (the descriptive sense), but our task is to become authentically or truly human (the prescriptive sense). When Merton talks about becoming human, he has this second meaning in mind. The twentieth-century mystic Simone Weil agrees. Although we're born human, authentic or fulfilled humanity is "absent" in most of us, "invisible" rather than manifest, nascent instead of actual. Our lifelong task is to cooperate with divine grace to transform our potential for genuine humanhood into a here-and-now reality. And when we do this, she concludes, we discover our saintliness.[5]

What's the fundamental quality of authentic humanhood we're called to cultivate? Scripture leaves no doubt about the answer: holiness. The word *holiness (qodesh)*, and its cognates *holy (qadosh)* and *sanctify (qiddesh)*, appear over six hundred times in the Hebrew Bible alone. Taken together, they provide a comprehensive description of God (or at least as comprehensive a one as we can grasp). In the biblical tradition, holiness isn't merely one divine attribute among others. Rather, it's the very essence of the Godhead: "Holy, holy, holy is the LORD of hosts" (Isaiah 6:3).

Although holiness originates with God, it isn't limited to God. All creation shimmers with divine holiness. The artwork bears the stamp of the Artist. The heavens and the earth, the stars and the seas and the sands, the humble insect and the proud lion—all reflect the radiant presence of the Holiness that crafted them. They do so, however, in a dumb, inarticulate way. Only one class of the world's inhabitants (so far as we know) is capable of consciously attuning to the holiness imparted to it in the act of creation: humans. Of all that is, we and we alone not only reflect God's holiness but are aware of doing so. This, surely, is part of what it means to be made in the "image" (Exodus 1:26) of God: the ability to recognize and celebrate the awesome fact that we participate in divine holiness.

But the word *holiness*, just like *human*, can be understood in either a descriptive or prescriptive sense. Our status as divinely created things means that our deepest spiritual core contains something of the holiness of the Creator. In one manner of speaking, then, we are already holy because we're born holy. "God's temple is holy," says St. Paul, "and that temple is you" (1 Corinthians 3:17). But holiness, like humanness, must be grown into. It must be recognized, gratefully accepted for the boon it is, and assiduously cultivated. Otherwise, we never achieve the final end for which we're created, and accordingly live more or less stunted, "could've-been" lives. Holiness, then, is not only the birth-gift bestowed on each of us from the moment of our creation; it's also the goal, the end, to which our existence is properly directed. It's both our most essential innate quality and our final and truest destination. God tells the ancient Hebrews: "Be holy, for I am holy" (Leviticus 11:45). Saint Peter repeats the injunction: "As he who called you is holy, be holy yourselves in all your conduct" (1 Peter 1:15), "become partakers of the divine nature" (2 Peter 1:4). Verses such as these express the scriptural insight that authentic humanhood entails a conscious choice of what one already is: holy.

None of us is ordinary, as C. S. Lewis observed,[6] although we often forget this and, in our forgetfulness, act all too ordinarily. Each of us is a holy reflection of divine Holiness, and thus are unimaginably extraordinary. A saint is nothing more—nothing less—than a person who recognizes and strives to live up to his or her holy humanness. This is our true end, and to settle for anything else is to forsake the abundant life for which we were created.

Holy Caring

It's all well and good to realize that our essential quality is holiness, derived from the holy God who created and sustains us, and that our ultimate flourishing depends on a conscious embrace of who we are. But if we go no further than this, we remain on a rather intellectual level, and sainthood is always a lived way of being rather than an abstract definition. So we must push on and try to understand in more concrete terms what it means to be holy.

Scripture appeals to a number of meanings to describe divine holiness: God's utter and unutterable fullness, his incomprehensible otherness, his goodness, his absolute purity. But the one that contains and preeminently expresses all of them is "loving-mercy" (*chesed* in the Hebrew Bible, *eleos* in the Christian). God's holiness most manifestly reveals itself in his ever-present solicitude for humans and his total dedication to our well-being. The primordial act of creation, the beneficent diminution of divine plenitude for the sake of bringing forth the world, is an act of holy love; the covenant with Abraham, the liberation of the Hebrews from Egyptian bondage, the raising up of ancient Israel's judges and kings and prophets, are additional expressions of this love; and the ultimate act of love is the sacrificial self-emptying of God in Christ for the salvation of humanity. To say that God is holy is first and foremost to say that God is loving. God, in fact, *is* Love, and therein lies God's resplendent holiness.

If we are to realize our destiny as partakers in divine holiness and thus become fully human, we must live as best we can God's loving-kindness by allowing its seed within us to blossom and reach out to both God and our fellows. As Dietrich Bonhoeffer wrote in one of his prison letters:

> God requires that we should love him eternally
> with our whole hearts, yet not so as to compro-
> mise or diminish our earthly affections, but as a
> kind of *cantus firmus* to which the other melodies
> of life provide the counterpoint.[7]

Learning to love so that our lives harmonize with the symphony of divine love that floods the universe: in this is our humanity, our holiness, our ultimate fulfillment as saints.

But a difficulty immediately arises. How can we way-ward and wounded humans love with anything like the intensity, the purity, the goodness, and the sacrifice of divine love? The obvious answer is that we can't. Unhappy experi-ence teaches us that even when we know the better, we do the worse. Our struggles to love generously and disinterest-edly (even supposing that we *do* struggle) sadly miss the mark. The harder we try, the more we seem to fail. Good intentions and earnest efforts fizzle to frustration, anxiety and, if we're not careful, cynicism or despair.

Much of the problem lies precisely in the fact that we strain mightily but not wisely. Contrary to the impression given by popular songs or romance novels, loving well and truly is the most difficult task any of us will ever undertake. It's a lifelong struggle, not an overnight *fait accompli*. It's some-thing we must work for, not suddenly fall into. Granted, we're born from holy Love and endowed with the talent for holy loving. Yet the talent must be nurtured and disciplined, and even then our attempts to love will never come close to the love God graciously extends to us. Saint Paul is fond of liken-ing the spiritual life to an athletic race (e.g., 1 Corinthians 9:26–27; Philippians 3:14; 2 Timothy 4:7). But would-be marathoners must prepare themselves through years of steady training before they take their place at the starting line. Simi-larly, when it comes to imitating God's love, we must learn to walk before we can hope to run. Sprinting down the track before we've toned our muscles is a foolishness that inevitably leads to spiritual cramps.

So for those of us who are beginners on the road to holiness—and that, of course, is most of us—a training regimen is in order. We would do well to follow the lead provided by C. A. Anderson Scott who, in a book on Christian ethics, recommends:

> We [can] guard ourselves against serious misunderstanding if in many passages of the New Testament we rendered the word "love" by "care." "Thou shalt care for the Lord thy God with all thy heart." "Thou shalt care for thy neighbor as thyself."[8]

Caring seems a modest act, particularly for those of us impatient to begin the race and cross the finish line. But it is and it isn't, and this is the secret of its effectiveness. Its modesty lies in the fact that caring is a possibility well within the reach of each of us. When contrasted with the high demands of loving, it's a little thing to do. Yet for all that, caring is the mighty centrifugal force that wears away the hard rind of a heart and opens it up to a genuinely saintly—a genuinely human—solicitude for oneself, others, and God. When we cultivate the habit of caring, we enter into a new relationship with reality, one that nudges us, albeit in a quiet and nondramatic manner, toward the holiness for which we were born.

The great truth that modest acts can lead imperceptibly to wondrous ends is nicely captured in an ancient Zen parable. A youthful greenhorn asks a Zen master to accept him as a disciple and teach him enlightenment. "Sure," the master replies. The new disciple eagerly expects that the old man will immediately initiate him into hidden mysteries, stuffing him full of esoteric truths and magical words. But to his surprise, he's told to go chop wood. When that's done, the youth is ordered to go down to the well and draw water. When he returns, he's given yet another menial task. This goes on for years and years. Instead of the secret teachings the young man expected, the old master assigns him one boringly mundane chore after another. At times, particularly in the beginning, the youth burns with resentment. But he's convinced that the master holds the key to enlightenment. So whenever he's tempted to throw in the towel, he suppresses his impatience in the hope that the real instruction will soon begin.

For nearly three decades this cycle of hard labor and frustrated expectation continues. Finally the old man lies dying, still without having revealed what the now middle-aged disciple so wants. So the disciple creeps softly up to the master's bed. *"Sansei,"* he whispers. "What about your promise to teach me the secret of enlightenment? For half a lifetime I've served you faithfully. What of your promise?"

The old man looks at the disciple and smiles. "Haven't you learned anything in all this time?" he asks. "When you first arrived here, you were impatient, demanding, restless, selfishly absorbed with lust for your own salvation. For twenty-five years I've taught you how to liberate yourself from these demons. Your service to me has given you the opportunity to cultivate self-forgetfulness, patience, loyalty, concern for another's well-being. What more would you have from me?" And when the disciple heard these words, he suddenly knew the joy of enlightenment. He became a saint.

Caring is very much like the regimen the Zen master put his overly eager student through. It involves a lifestyle that sometimes appears quite irrelevant to the goal of realizing one's holiness and becoming fully human. There are generally no flashy breakthrough moments when it comes to caring, no opportunities for Hollywoodish daring-do or momentous sacrifice. Instead, caring cultivates holiness in a cumulative, often scarcely noticeable fashion. In this regard, it's very much like the "little way" practiced and taught by Thérèse of Lisieux, one that calls for faithful attentiveness to the "small" things of life. Thérèse realized that the only proper way to achieve holiness was "to remain little and become this more and more,"[9] and this at least requires the patience to forgo the temptation to run before we've learned to walk. Again, a modest sounding goal. But like the disciple in the Zen parable, the person who has learned to care discovers at the end of the day that genuine caring unobtrusively but surely sanctifies and fulfills one's existence. We will never be able to love as God loves, but we *can* care. And as Godlike creatures rather than gods, that's good enough.

Saying that caring is the "little" way to sainthood shouldn't lead us to suspect that it's easy or even particularly pleasant. Keep in mind the story of the Zen disciple. What he wanted was a thrillingly flamboyant route to salvation. What he got was something quite different: backbreaking drudgery at menial and frequently dirty tasks, mundane routine, apparently thankless service—exactly the sort of humdrum round he hoped to avoid by going to the Zen master. What he finally discovered, however, was that the very life he tried to escape was exactly what he needed, and that what initially seemed a burden and curse eventually proved to be a blessing.

Genuine caring similarly brings great joy and fulfillment, but along the way it can be tedious and downright painful. It reveals dark facts about ourselves we may have spent a lifetime avoiding, facts likely to humiliate and even break us when we finally face them. It requires us to place ourselves willingly in the service of others, and to share their sorrowful wounds even when we'd much rather be doing something more pleasant. It forces us to throw away our tinny idols, that pantheon of user-friendly gods we worship out of laziness and fear and pride, and crackle in the consuming flames of the one holy and inscrutable God.

No, there's nothing easy about learning to care. Like all training regimens, caring is medicinal, and medicines often bring discomfort before they start to restore health. So we need to be positive that we want the cure before we lift the bottle to our lips. John's Gospel reminds us of this with the story of Jesus' healing of the lame man at the pool of Bethsatha (see John 5:6). Before Jesus lays hands upon the man, he asks a curious question, a disconcerting question: Are you sure, quite sure, you wish to be healed? Are you sure, quite sure, you're willing to practice walking so that eventually you may run? What an absurd question! Of course anyone who's lame wants to be healed! But Jesus well understood the deeper implications of what was going on. He knew that learning to walk in the way of caring is more difficult than most of us who narrowly fix our gaze on the finish line can possibly imagine. But he also knew it to be a necessary training for the eventual sprint to humanness and holiness.

LEARNING TO CARE

This book plumbs more deeply the holy caring that little by little pushes us ever closer to sainthood. Reading about caring is obviously no substitute for rolling up one's sleeves and actually doing it, but it can help us make a start. My hope is that the exploration offered here can serve in some small way to aid in the recognition and embrace of your (and my) destiny as a saint.

Growth into holy caring, like any kind of spiritual development, demands discernment on our part. In a haunting and beautiful poem-prayer, T. S. Eliot makes this petition: "Teach us to care and not to care."[10] Exactly. Genuine care rests on wisely discriminating between those things worthy of care and those that aren't. Most of our failures at caring are ultimately traceable to an inability to distinguish between the two. Moreover, we're often confused about the actual meaning of the word *care*, mistaking it for mere sentimentality or gushy emotional overflows or suffocating over-protection.

This suggests that learning to care is a dynamic process that involves both negation and affirmation. We must first negate—*un*know, or *un*learn—before we can affirm—know, or learn. Seed can't be planted or harvested in unbroken or weed-choked earth. In the case of caring, what must be unlearned are false notions of how to care and what to care for. Only after this undergrowth is cleared can we hope to get a sense of what else grows there.

Chapter 1 begins to till the soil by offering an analysis of the deep meaning of the word *care*. We'll discover that genuine caring isn't a psychological state or an emotional mood so much as a spiritual attentiveness that transforms our being and, in the process, reconfigures our relationship with the self, other persons, and God.

We have an unfortunate tendency, born of fears, insecurities, and confused self-will, to think of ourselves as mere things living in a universe of things. The fall into thinghood alienates us from the recognition that we and the reality in which we dwell shimmer with a divinely bestowed vitality that can never be reduced to the dumb inertness of thinghood. This vitality is what I call *presence*. Caring is a celebratory embrace of the presence that radiates from ourselves, from other persons, and preeminently from God. When we attune to it, we begin to live as presences capable of entering into deep communion with the presence of others as well as the Presence of God. Consequently, caring is an inward movement (toward one's true self) and an outward movement (toward others and God), and both of them nudge us ever closer toward full humanness. But because our habit of "thinging" the world is so ingrained, the impetus for caring is necessarily a grace-gift, a divinely initiated puncture of the defensive shell in which we enclose ourselves and stifle our spiritual growth. We can prepare ourselves for the decisive moment when God graciously cracks open our hardened hearts to alert us to presence, and we can cooperate with that moment when it comes. But we do not and cannot forge ahead on our own steam.

This understanding of caring as a way of being that opens us to presence sets the stage for a more detailed exploration of what it means to care for one's self (chapter 2), for our sisters and brothers (chapter 3), and for God (chapter 4).

Care for self involves moving away from the everyday "me" upon which we normally fix our attention and energies, thereby falling into the bondage of thinghood, and focusing instead on that mysteriously vital stillpoint of the soul that reflects and participates in divine Presence and constitutes our true identity. When we do this, we're liberated to embrace our nobility as creatures stamped with the unerasable imprint of God. We also find the self-affirmation and courage to be human.

Learning to care for self brings freedom and self-insight. Only after we've learned to recognize and care for the true self can we learn to recognize and care for our fellows as well. This is the next transformative stage of caring. The world encourages us to view others either as threats to our well-being or pawns to be manipulated in the pursuit of our goals.

But the discovery of our own true identity awakens us to the fact that others are also bearers of the divine Presence, and this leads us to appreciate them for the noble Christ-selves they are. We realize our hearts are linked to theirs, and we freely—joyfully—reach out to share their wounds, affirm their strengths, ease their burdens, nonjudgmentally nurture their growth into humanness, and offer them in return the gift of our own vulnerability and joy.

Learning to care for others gifts us with compassion and community.

Finally, this caring recognition of self and others frees us to enter into a new and more enriching relationship with God himself. Just as caring allows us to jettison confusions that blind us to our own nature and the natures of others, so it likewise liberates us from "religious" delusions that stand in the way of genuine connection with God, the supreme Presence who pulsates throughout creation and rescues it from dumb thinghood. Caring for God is a receptivity that seeks neither to penetrate and tame the impenetrable Mystery he is, nor to sidestep that Mystery by clutching at convenient but unworthy substitutes. Caring for God is a willingness to become increasingly available to the mysterious Presence who graciously saturates the universe with himself, and to consent to that Presence by incarnating it as best we can in our own lives.

Learning to care for God allows us to enter with humble awe and joyful gratitude into the unfathomable mystery of God.

When we begin to walk the transformative path of holy caring, in short, we grow in self-insight, enter into compassionate community with others, and celebrate God: all necessary steps in our spiritual evolution toward humanness.

Or, as Graham Greene would say, toward sainthood.

1

SIMEON'S RIDDLE

To live in the present is to live in the Presence: to see God in all things and to see all things, all situations, all moments, all interests and desires, in Him.

—Gerald Vann

A MYSTERIOUS ENCOUNTER

There are many strange tales recorded in Hebrew and Christian Scripture: the burning bush in the Midian wilderness, Saul's eerie rendezvous with the witch of Endor, Lazarus's hair-raising return from the shadows, the firestorm at Pentecost. But no story is quite so uncanny as the prophecy of Simeon recorded in Luke's Gospel (see 2:22–35).

Mary and Joseph, following the religious practice of their day, have taken the infant Jesus to Jerusalem to consecrate him to Yahweh. The occasion is solemn but also joyful. On the one hand, the new parents are unsettled by the awesome significance of their child's formal presentation at the Temple—an infant, mind you, whose conception and birth have already thrust the parents into a frightening awareness of his uniqueness. On the other hand, Mary and Joseph are aglow both with proud delight in their son and the festive excitement that accompanies any visit to David's holy city. Emotions are mixed, nerves stretched taut.

The young mother carries her baby into the noisy temple courtyard, straining against the crowd, protectively shielding her son from the tumultuous ocean of worshipers and money-changers and merchants gathered there. She's a country girl, brought up in the quiet of a backwoods village, and she finds the hubbub of the Temple rather overwhelming. Just as she reaches the portico to the second courtyard and breathes a sigh of relief, an old man breaks from the crowd, steps in front of her, and gestures for the infant. Mary freezes; there's something alarming about the look in the stranger's eyes. But she finds herself unable to resist his silent command, and apprehensively hands over the baby. The old man lifts the child heavenward and in curiously exulted tones begins to chant a thanks-offering to Yahweh:

> Lord, now lettest thou thy servant depart in peace,
>   according to thy word;
> for mine eyes have seen thy salvation
> which thou hast prepared in the presence of all
>   peoples,
> a light for revelation to the Gentiles,
> and for glory to thy people Israel!

The old man holds the infant close to his dim eyes, peering hungrily into its face for some time, before finally returning Jesus to Mary. Then he leans in close to her, fixes her in his gaze, and whispers words that chill her soul and haunt her for the rest of her days.

> Behold, this child is set for the fall and rising of
>   many in Israel,
> and for a sign that is spoken against
> (and a sword will pierce through your own soul
>   also),
> that thoughts out of many hearts may be revealed.

Familiarity doesn't necessarily breed contempt, but it can encourage dullness. We've all heard the *Nunc dimittis* story so frequently—at least once a year, at Christmastide—that we may have become inured to its sheer weirdness. But if we make an effort to read it with fresh eyes, we can't but be struck by how eerie it is. A total (and seemingly lunatic) stranger shoves his way into what properly ought to be a private celebratory moment, and in a single breath both raises a young mother's hopes for her child and freezes her heart with a terrifying oracle of doom and misery. This dissonance is what makes Simeon's speech so unsettling: exuberant gratitude for the arrival of the promised Messiah coupled with an ominous prediction that the child will somehow do damage to many, including its own mother. Salvific revelation, devastating sorrow: Simeon insists that the one will necessarily accompany the other. The resulting incongruence is, to say the least, disturbing.

Most of what Simeon says in the first part of his prophecy seems straightforward enough: Jesus has been brought into the world to redeem humankind, Jew and Gentile alike, even though his good news will be rejected by some and embraced by others. But the final two lines of the prophecy pose a riddle that has perplexed commentators for centuries. What's the sword that will thrust through Mary? What does Simeon mean when he predicts that it will also expose the heart's deepest secrets of many others? Grappling with the meaning of these two mysterious pronouncements will start us on our way to an understanding of holy caring. For Simeon knows the secret to becoming fully human. Prophet that he is, however, he refuses to speak it outright, knowing too well that such truths must be experienced and lived before they can be appreciated.

THE SWORD IN THE HEART

Ancient commentators were divided in their interpretations of Simeon's oracular warning.[1] The Eastern Fathers, following the third-century Origen, tended to see the sword as a metaphor for doubt. On this reading, the blade that slices through Mary is bewildered incredulity at her son's later claim to Godhood, and her despairing loss of hope during the passion and death of Jesus. The inmost thought laid bare by the sword is lack of faith, the failure to accept wholeheartedly the tidings that Jesus truly is Immanuel, God-with-us. The same doubt that pierced Mary prior to the Resurrection also wounds all subsequent generations who, likewise, hear but can't or won't accept the good news.

The Latin Fathers by and large rejected this interpretation. For them, the sword was better understood as a metaphor for sorrow: the anguish felt by a mother who helplessly watches as her beloved son is reviled, tortured, and executed. On this reading, the inmost thought revealed by the sorrowful sword is a mystical connection, first in Mary and then in all believers, with Christ's passion. This exegesis of Simeon's prophecy became the conventional one in the West, eventually culminating in the popular and officially sanctioned devotion to the seven *dolors* or sorrows of Mary.[2]

Although it's rash to deny the value of either of these attempts to crack Simeon's riddle, it's also the case that neither is wholly satisfying. The Eastern Church's presumption that Mary had misgivings about Jesus' claim to divinity simply lacks scriptural warrant. The sword of doubt obviously pierces the hearts of most believers at one time or another, but there's no evidence that it ever assailed Mary. The Latin Church's claim that the sword symbolizes sorrow is more loyal to the scriptural record, but it tends to conflate the weapon that lays bare the soul's inmost thoughts with those inmost thoughts themselves, leading to the awkward redundancy of sorrow revealing sorrow. So the prophecy remains enigmatic, leaving us with the same questions that puzzled ancient commentators.

I'd like to suggest that we can come to a better understanding of Simeon's riddle, especially as it sheds light on the meaning of holy caring, if we examine more carefully its three central terms: heart, sword, and inmost thoughts.

Heart: Simeon says that Jesus' coming is somehow connected with a sword that will pierce the soul/heart of both Mary and many others. In New Testament Greek, *soul,* or *psyche,* and *heart,* or *kardia,* are, for the most part, interchangeable. Luke, probably to avoid a stylistically clumsy repetition, employs both words in recording Simeon's prophecy.

Why the heart? Obviously the heart is the source of physical life, the organ responsible for the maintenance of our physical being. For both the Jews and the Greeks (and for us today, at least in a metaphorical sense), it was also the center of spiritual vitality. Biologically speaking, the heart pumps blood, the essence of organic life, throughout the body. But from a religious perspective, the heart is that sacred cave of mystery where divine nature and human nature meet—where God, says St. Paul, has poured himself (see Romans 5:5)—and thus is a divinely charged battery that ceaselessly quickens the spirit. "Find the door of your heart," advises John Chrysostom, and "you will discover it is the door of the Kingdom of God."[3] Physiological characteristics define us in only an accidental way. We can, after all, lose limbs or senses without ceasing to be who we are. But the heart's mysterious linkage of us and the Divine grounds our true nature. To lose it is to lose everything; to grow dull to it is to lapse into a less-than-human state.

Because heart is the place where God is, it's the seat of insight. Insight is the ability to recall truths we've always known but for one reason or another have forgotten—truths, as the Psalmist says (see 119:11), embedded deeply within us. Moreover, the heart is the center of will and purpose (see Deuteronomy 8:2; Jeremiah 23:20), and to "incline the heart" (Psalm 119:36) is to consent "wholeheartedly" to the truths that repose in it. Finally, the heart is also the seat of judgment, that integrative black box that translates divine wisdom and moral insight—God's law (see Isaiah 51:7)—into terms the human intellect can comprehend. To recall the moral wisdom buried deep in the core of who we are and then incline the will to it is to walk in the way of righteousness (see 1 John 3:19–20). Conversely, to harden one's heart is either to ignore the wisdom hidden at the center of our being or to rebel against it. Such recalcitrance is not just self-destructively foolish. It's also the origin of evil. Pharaoh sets his heart against the children of Israel (see Exodus 10:20, 11:10), and his ultimate downfall is the direct consequence of his sinful defiance of divine direction.

When Simeon speaks of the heart, then, he's referring to that mysterious spiritual core within each person that constitutes his or her deepest, truest being, and from which flow the reflective will, intelligence, and moral sensitivity that distinguish us from brutes. Since heart is the place where God is present, it also establishes an unbreakable link between us and the Creator. As John Donne wrote in the seventeenth century, "the heart of man is an epitome of God's great booke . . . , and man need no farther looke."[4] This linkage is horizontal as well as vertical: the presence of God that pulsates within each of us is the common thread that binds all human hearts together and allows for the possibility of communion between persons. When we heed our heart stirrings and incline our wills to their whisperings, we gain insight into our own true natures as well as our innate connectedness with God and other humans. For the heart, as one of the ancient desert fathers put it, is the inner cell that "shall teach thee all things."[5]

Sword: The problem, as Scripture has already suggested to us, is that we have a tendency to deafen ourselves to the call of the heart. Instead of following the lead of the Spirit that dwells within us, we harden the heart and focus on our egoistic drives, ambitions, yearnings, aggressions, and fears. Like mighty Pharaoh, the incessant clamor of our own will deafens us to the gentle heart-murmuring of God's presence.

Both the Hebrew and the Christian Scriptures can be read as records of this refusal to harken to God and thereby touch base with our deepest spiritual core. The primordial Edenic couple set the ball in motion by substituting their egoistic judgments for heart-truth, the children of the covenant hardened their hearts against God and hurtled into Egyptian bondage, and the post-Exodus kings and commoners of Israel forgot the hard-won lessons of the wilderness and closed themselves off from the stirrings of heart-wisdom. Each of the Hebrew prophets takes as his mandate the thankless task of reawakening people to the great insight that God dwells within, and each of them frequently invokes the heart-metaphor to get across his message. Isaiah laments that Israel's heart has arrogantly pulled away from God (see 29:13); Jeremiah plaintively begs Jerusalem to wash her heart clean of polluting self-will (see 4:14); Daniel thunders that awful judgment awaits those who refuse to humble their hearts (see 5:22).

Jesus takes up the metaphor in the Christian Scriptures. In the Sermon on the Mount, for example, he lists purity or openness of heart as one of the beatitudes (see Matthew 5:8), and repeats Isaiah's lamentation that most hearts close themselves to God (see Matthew 15:8). In a similar vein, the author of Acts observes that even after the resurrection and Pentecost events, the people's hearts grew dull, their ears heavy, their eyes dim (see 28:27). The author of Hebrews uses the same image by imploring the early Christians not to harden their hearts to the good news (see 4:7).

The conclusion suggested by the biblical record is that the human heart has the unhappy tendency to encrust itself with layer upon layer of stubborn self-will. As the layers accumulate, awareness of the divine core, our true being, gradually diminishes until it's all but forgotten. Our hearts petrify until we're powerless to halt the ossification on our own, even if we wished to do so, and we fall from the vitality of humanness to dead thinghood.

Paul's epistle to the Romans takes this inability to chisel a way out of our stony self-imprisonment as its central theme. The Law is no help here. Even if we somehow open ourselves long enough to take notice of the commandments, the killing habit of self-will has become so entrenched that we can't muster the discipline to truly honor them, to be genuine "doers" rather than just indifferent or self-serving "hearers" of the Law (see Romans 2:13). We may manage a rough and ready outward conformity to the Law, but unless our response comes from the heart, even punctilious observance counts for little. Genuine fidelity to the Law, says Paul, "is a matter of the heart, spiritual and not literal" (Romans 2:29), and our closure of the heart forestalls such interiority: "All have sinned and fall short of the glory of God" (Romans 3:23). It requires but little reflection on our own lives to show us that Paul's indictment is neither peevish theology nor gloomy pessimism. It's simply a statement of sorry fact. Despite our conceit of righteousness, we're giants trapped in chunks of dead stone, and all the struggling and straining in the world can't free us.

What force is powerful enough to slice through an imprisoned heart and emancipate the life locked away in it? Obviously not an act of unaided bootstrapping, a clench-jawed determination, however resolute, to mend our ways. This is Paul's dismal insight. Nor will mere conformity to the Law melt a stony heart, any more than intellectual mastery of various ethical theories. Pharisees and philosophers are just as susceptible to spiritual petrification as anyone else.

Serious maladies require drastic measures, and Simeon offers one with his image of a razor-edged sword—and not just any sword, either. The Greek term Luke uses is *rhomphaia,* the large Thracian broadsword notorious in the ancient world for its fierceness. A *rhomphaia* was an offensive weapon, a huge blade wielded with two hands, whose sharpness and weight were formidable. Helmets and shields and armor were effec-tive against lesser swords, but offered little if any protection against a *rhomphaia* blow. Simeon suggests that the same thing goes for a hardened heart: although it might withstand other weapons, it must fall before the *rhomphaia.*

The full significance of Simeon's *rhomphaia* becomes clear once we realize that the term is found in only one other scrip-tural context. When the New Testament authors wrote about swords, the word they typically preferred was *machaira,* the short thrusting blade of the Roman legionary. Although obvi-ously a good weapon, the *machaira* was second-class when matched with the heftier *rhomphaia.* The single other place in the Bible where *rhomphaia* appears instead of *machaira* is the Book of Revelation. There, John uses *rhomphaia* to designate the messianic sword issuing from Christ's mouth, the mighty blade with which the triumphant Christ cuts down God's foes (cf. Revelation 1:16; 2:12).

The message behind both Luke's and John's imagery is that the one weapon capable of slicing through a hardened heart is God's Word (it's significant that Revelation describes the *rhomphaia* as coming out of Christ's *mouth*), the Word made incarnate two thousand years ago, the Word ever incarnate in the deepest recesses of the human heart. God's historic self-disclosure in Jesus the Christ is an outward sign of God's continuous self-disclosure in the heart. The *rhomphaia* thrust that pierces the heart and enables us to consciously discern the Word pulsating there comes from within, stabbing outward until the stony carapace finally cracks and shatters. As Karl Barth pointed out in one of his sermons, divine revelation is "the opening of a door [that] can be unlocked only from the inside."[6] God's sword/Word has always been embedded in the heart as a sort of spiritual failsafe to recall us from our neglectful forgetfulness. But it's only with the historically visible manifestation of the Word, Jesus, that we fully awaken to the presence of the corresponding interior one. This is what the aged Simeon realized when he spied the messianic infant in the temple courtyard: here, finally, was the long-awaited Gift, graciously bestowed by God, that would release the Word trapped within the frozen heart and liberate men and women from bondage.

The sword that liberates God from the stubbornly recalcitrant heart is God himself.

Inmost thoughts: Simeon says that when the sword of God's Word graciously opens the heart, the blow discloses many *dialogismoi kardion,* which may be rendered as "inmost thoughts," "thoughts out of the heart," or "heart-thoughts." However we translate it, the expression's import is clear enough: *dialogismoi kardion* are divinely seeded truths about reality deeply buried in the hardened heart and subsequently forgotten. But when the sword bisects the heart, these truths are unconcealed to and for us. What was hidden in cavernous darkness is illuminated by divine light, and we remember what we knew all along.

Ancient as well as modern biblical scholars have often offered another interpretation: that *dialogismoi kardion* are those self-destructive urges that fuel our egoistic wills and deflect us from spiritual growth. The searchlight of the Word hunts down these creatures of the night, routing them from their lairs and forcing them into the open. Selfishness, obstinacy, tremulous fears, and vaunting pride—all responsible for the petrification of the heart—are revealed as the deformities they are. The person who has had his or her inmost and dirtiest secrets uncovered is then faced with the awesome opportunity of either repudiating or hanging onto them.

The claim that *dialogismoi kardion* are thoughts hostile to the Word of God is a reasonable one. After all, Simeon's prophecy suggests this dark interpretation when it proclaims that God's sword/Word is a sign that will be rejected by many, thus leading to their spiritual downfall. One is reminded here of what Jesus later says about Pharisaic hypocrisy: "Nothing is covered up that will not be revealed; nothing is hidden that will not be made known" (Luke 12:2). Given the context in which this sentence is spoken, Jesus' point clearly is that what will be revealed is hidden evil. When the divine sword cuts open the heart, the poison within it spurts out for even the most obtuse to see.

But we've noted that the heart is that mysterious place within men and women that houses the divine Spirit. So the inmost thoughts revealed when the sword pierces the heart can't be just those shameful passions that blind us to the indwelling presence of God; they must also include an awareness of that presence, and all that it entails. Simeon acknowledges this, too, in his prophecy: the unconcealed *dialogismoi kardion* will lead to the downfall of many in

Israel, but also to the *rising* of many. The heart, recall, is the seat of insight, the repository of spiritual truths that we always know but frequently forget. The sword that passes through the heart brings these truths back to consciousness. So at the very instant that the sword spotlights the self-imposed obstacles that block us from embracing our Godlike nature and fulfilling our destiny as humans, it also opens us to a living awareness of the brilliant nature of that destiny.

Saint Paul was correct: the temple *is* the dwelling place of God, and the heart is that temple. As the poet George Herbert put it some fifteen centuries later, "Jesu is in my heart, the sacred name/Is deeply carved there."[7] When we enter into the temple's holy of holies, we stand before the unutterable name that reveals everything, the good as well as the bad, the sacred and the profane, our blemished actual past but also our spotless potential future. All is unconcealed, nothing remains hidden. Yet in order to enter this sanctuary, the temple veil must first be rent by God. He does this with the mighty *rhomphaia* of his Word, thereby revealing both himself and our own true natures. God the revealer, God *and* humanity the revelation. Darkness gives way to light:

> If his Word once teach us, shoot a ray
> Through all the heart's dark chambers, and reveal
> Truths undiscerned but by that holy light,
> Then all is plain.[8]

PRESENCE

Simeon's riddle offers astute albeit veiled insight into the means of becoming human. The problem is that our twentieth-century vocabulary is different from Simeon's. References to the heart-cavern, the liberating sword of divine grace, and the indwelling Word revealed by that sword may be too arcanely "churchy" for our secularized sensibilities to fully appreciate.

Fortunately, however, spiritual teachings are amazingly accommodating. Their truth remains eternal but is communicable in the fluid idioms of any age and culture. So to bore deeper into Simeon's meaning, I'd like to translate his language into terms more familiar to the twentieth-century ear. These terms are *alienation* on the one hand and *authenticity* on the other. Those who have hardened their hearts suffer from the blight of spiritual alienation, while those whose hearts have been opened by grace begin to live authentically. As we'll see, the hallmark of an alienated existence is self-enclosed bondage and forlornness, whereas the chief characteristic of authentic existence is an opening of the heart that leads to fulfillment.

Alienated bondage: The term *alienation* is bandied about so frequently and in so many contexts that its meaning has become rather diffuse. But regardless of when and where it's used, the word always carries a negative connotation, implying a state of suffocating estrangement in which we endure isolated and helpless frustration.

All of us have felt the bite of alienation at one time or another in our lives. Perhaps we've been stuck in a dead-end job that stifled creative self-expression. In this case, we talk about being "alienated" from our work. Maybe we've offered our hearts to another person only to have our love rebuffed or even cruelly betrayed. In this case, to use a rather old-fashioned expression, we say that our affections have been "alienated." Or perhaps we've found ourselves in a new country filled with persons and customs totally foreign to us. We've felt acutely out of place and almost unbearably uncomfortable because the situation is so "alien" to what we're used to. Each of these experiences of alienation has one thing in common: they shut us off from liberating possibilities, imprisoning us in environments that stymie personal development. Alienation is a form of enslavement. It freezes us into the status of things: entities that have no future, no obvious prospect of change or self-direction, because of our domination by hostile external circumstances.

The alienation that can be inflicted by dissatisfying work, unhappy love affairs, and bafflingly strange environments is horrible enough. But it doesn't come close to the miserable estrangement Simeon alludes to in his prophecy. That alienation is spiritual rather than circumstantial: the frustrated imprisonment of a hardened heart, a heart so shut down by self-imposed thinghood that it takes the jolt of God's *rhomphaia* to jumpstart it. Alienation from work or the beloved or the environment is devastating, but it need not mean the end of us. Individuals afflicted by these types of alienation might just manage to keep their heads above water—although, admittedly, it's an ordeal to do so—if they have strong inner resources to call upon. As the apostle Paul pointed out, external constraints, although not to be trivialized, don't necessarily shackle a free spirit (see 1 Corinthians 7:12–24). But persons suffering from a hardened heart are their own source of enslavement. Their bondage can't be chalked up to distressing external circumstances. Instead, it originates deeply within themselves. They have nothing to fall back on because they've separated themselves from the indwelling source of life. They've forsworn their own possibilities and hence exiled themselves to the kingdom of things.

The estrangement of a hardened heart is the spiritual

cancer that attacks us when we willfully close ourselves off from the Word within and thus forget who we are. The ensuing rupture between our true nature and the stunted thing we become hurtles us along a deadly path that takes us further and further away from the possibility of genuine humanness. Progressively beset with frustration, anxiety, abandonment, and a general sense of lostness, the alienated self is unable to find a comfortable niche in the world, stymied from entering into communion with other persons or with God, and derives no real satisfaction, much less joy, from life. Handicapped by forgetfulness, preoccupied with chronic frustration, it—and I use the term "it" deliberately—loses the capacity to open up to anything that makes life worth living.

Spiritual alienation, then, is a state of radical discontinuity between what we're destined to be and what we become when we substitute our will for God's. It's a plunge into subhuman thinghood, a devolution that makes us strangers to ourselves, our fellow humans, and the Divine, a fall from freedom to slavery. We become futureless objects cast on a barren landscape, and our misery is unbearable.

Even worse, the misery is of our own making. As we've already seen, we sometimes experience alienation through no fault of our own by being trapped in unrewarding jobs, unhappy love affairs, or confusingly strange environments. But spiritual alienation isn't an estrangement forced on us by external circumstances. Rather, it's a self-willed rejection of our God-given possibilities as humans. This means that spiritual alienation isn't merely destructive; it's also sinful. Centuries ago, Isaac of Stella wrote that in creating us, God graciously commanded us to live, to be.[9] "To *be*—for this God created all," as Wisdom says (1:14, Jerusalem Bible, emphasis added). Yet the alienated self rebelliously refuses to grow into the gift of human being. It hardens the heart, deafens itself to the Word within, and chooses a course of stubborn self-determination that pits its own misguided wishes and shortsighted judgments against God's plan and wisdom. The alienated self perversely repudiates the offer of being and, in doing so, disobeys God's primal commandment to be. In his play "No Exit," Jean-Paul Sartre famously proclaims that "hell is other people."[10] But when it comes to spiritual alienation, Sartre's mistaken. Hell isn't other people; it's the agony of refusing God's invitation to full being.

Liberating authenticity: Simeon's riddle suggests that our last and best chance of breaking the chains of spiritual alienation is the outward thrust of God's *rhomphaia*. Left to its own devices, the alienated self is powerless to crack the shell that estranges it from humanness. But when the sword of God goes through the heart, it unconceals both the horribly blighted corruption of the alienated self and the shimmering promise of its destined identity. Awareness of sin brings with it the possibility of moving from alienation to fulfillment, to an authentic way of being, as Paul Tillich observes, in which self-estrangement is overcome and through which we enter into "a reality of reconciliation and reunion, of creativity, meaning and hope."[11] No right-thinking person would cling to a state of miserable thinghood when offered a way out, especially when the reward—complete realization of one's human potential—is so attractive.

But what is this authentic way of being to which the divine sword invites us? Briefly, it's the "reconciliation and reunion," to use Tillich's phrase, that occurs when we freely choose our inherent Godlikeness, revealed to us by the flashing sword/Word. The Spirit that dwells within the heart is both our origin and our lodestone. It's the cause of our very existence as well as the identity we're summoned to grow into.

When we cease our destructively alienating rebellion and pay attention to this insight graciously revealed by the sword, our hitherto recalcitrant will begins to parallel the divine will. The Godlikeness that lay dormant in the hardened heart now blossoms into actuality, and we grow more and more like the Word that births and sustains us. We become increasingly reconciled and reunited with what we always were, and the rupture of alienation proportionately diminishes.

This openness to our deep Godlikeness reveals to us that the being to which we're called is not thinghood but "presence." To live authentically—to live Godly, to live *humanly*—is to acknowledge and embrace oneself as presence.

What is it to be a "presence"? The word comes from the Latin *praesens,* which in turn is a compound of *prae* and *sensus*. *Prae* is a prefix that carries meanings of "before," "in front of," "on account of," and "through," while *sensus* generally refers to "a capacity for feeling" (to be "sensitive") and "meaning" (as in the "sense" of something). A "presence," then, is that which is immediately and undeniably real and goes out of its way to disclose itself ("before" or "in front of" us), conveys meaning ("sense"), and awakens a response ("capacity for feeling").

God is the supreme Presence who makes possible all instances of presence. Rudolf Otto's description of divine Presence has become classic: *mysterium tremendum et fascinans.*[12] When we encounter God, we stand before a Reality so overwhelmingly present to us, so immediately and undeniably here-and-now, that we quake with fascinated awe, simultaneously unnerved but irresistibly attracted by its sheer Is-ness. All of us have run across men or women with such dynamic personalities that we feel slightly dizzy around them. They fill whatever room they enter. They seem larger than life, exuding a crackling vitality that unmistakably announces their presence, and when they depart, the room somehow seems forlornly empty. But the strong sense of reality we experience when we meet such individuals only dimly reflects the powerful impact of standing before the living God. In an encounter with the divine Presence, we know beyond any doubt that we've touched base with the ultimately Real—with what IS, here and now, past and future, as Moses discovered on Mount Horeb (see Exodus 3:14)—and everything else seems mere shadow in comparison.

Moreover, this Presence is supremely personal. Otherwise, an encounter with it would do nothing more than paralyze us with a horrible sense of absolutely alien otherness. It's true that when we stand before divine Presence we experience a *frisson* of hair-raising uncanniness. What figure in the Hebrew and the Christian Scriptures has ever met God and not been bowled over with fear and trembling? But the recurrent message heard by those who meet Presence is: "Be not afraid!" God isn't an impersonal cosmic force, a blind hurricane that blows through the universe without rhyme or reason. When Yahweh thunders his name on Mount Horeb, he significantly speaks not in metaphysical abstractions but in the first person: "*I* AM." The God who supremely IS is also that indescribably intimate Reality who makes himself available to us out of loving compassion, and when we stand before him we fill with a joyfully grateful awareness of his beneficent self-giving that tempers our fear and trembling. We sense that this ultimately real Presence is attracted to us, seeks us out, and carefully oversees our best interests, even if the solicitude at times is inscrutable or even terrifying.

In addition, the breathtakingly real and personally intimate Presence which God is strikes us as supremely meaningful, despite the fact that we find it impossible to pin a satisfactory name or adequate definition to it. We can label and classify realities—objects, events, ideas—but Reality itself mystifyingly eludes rational comprehension. Yet for all our inability to fathom its depths, we know with absolute certainty that divine Presence is the Meaning that showers meaning on our lives, and the Being that bestows being upon us. We cannot speak that Meaning without stumbling over words—but we can and do experience it in an immediate, living way. Our tongues are tied not because the encounter is absurd, but because the Meaning it conveys is so plenitudinous that it transcends our limited talents of analysis or expression.

Finally, divine Presence is supremely creative, irresistibly eliciting from us the responsive longing to participate ever more deeply in the reality, intimacy, and meaning we sense in it. The sculptor Michelangelo once said that he didn't impose shape on raw slabs of marble so much as he allowed the forms within the rock to discover and reveal themselves. His mallet and chisel only liberated the hidden potential in the marble. Similarly, divine Presence is a creative blowing upon our souls that awakens and releases the trace elements of Presence with which we're born. When we feel the wind of God blow through us, we yearn to make ourselves worthy of it by breathing the spirit of creative Presence upon and through the rough marble of our fellow humans.

God, then, is the Presence who reveals himself as the supremely meaningful yet mysterious "I AM," who suffuses us with a sense of profoundly intimate availability and solicitude, and who evokes in us a grateful and joyous longing to be creative conduits of the meaning we've experienced. This Presence is the Word that dwells in the heart and ceaselessly echoes throughout our being. It is the eternal Christ who made himself manifest two millennia ago so that we might discover the Word already implanted within us. And this Presence is also the flashing *rhomphaia* that opens the marbled heart to release our humanness.

This brings us back to the nature of authentic liberation. We are made in God's image, and our destiny is to so attune ourselves to what we are that we steadily grow in our likeness to God. "Be one with the Father," Jesus told the disciples, "as I am one with you" (see John 14:10; 17:21). Don't succumb to spiritual alienation's forgetfulness of the indwelling Presence and subsequent fall into thinghood. Allow your wills to gratefully consent to God's so that the heart can open to the unimaginably rich possibilities that are your birthright. This is what it means to become a human, to move from sinful alienation to authentic fulfillment. This is what it means to be free.

Now, we've seen that the God who is both our origin and goal is absolute Presence. It follows, then, that the life to which humans made in the divine image are called is a steadily swelling imitation of divine Presence. As Gerald Vann says in the epigraph to this chapter, an authentic human reflects the transcendent fullness, availability, intimacy, meaningfulness, and creativity of Presence in the here and now of the present. These qualities are the wonderful gifts planted in the heart, the *dialogismoi kardian* unconcealed for us by the swordthrust. They are the answers to Simeon's riddle.

CARE AS PRESENCING

But what does any of this have to do with caring? In a word: everything. For presence is the essence of caring. Caring, in fact, *is* presencing. To care is holy because it's an intentional imitation of divine Presencing. To care is to make oneself available, as God makes himself available, in a meaningful, intimate, and creative way, to one's deepest nature, to other humans, and ultimately to God himself. To care is to embrace and celebrate the Presence that percolates throughout existence, and in doing so to assent to *be*. To care is to become fully human.

If it seems strange to speak of caring as an assent to being, it's because we live in an age that rushes to collapse spiritual truths into psychological categories. Our modern sensibilities are uncomfortable with the arcane language of theology and metaphysics. Rather, we prefer to use the more familiar discourse of psychology—even pop psychology—when it comes to talking about caring. So what do we do? We reduce caring to a predictable set of feelings or emotions accompanied by a socially prescribed pattern of behavioral responses. When we feel care, we experience solicitous, sorrowful, affectionate, or pitying emotions. When we act caringly, we hug, stroke, hand-hold, or encourage.

Now, I don't for a moment want to claim that these interpretations of caring are illegitimate. No person in her right mind would deny that caring has an emotional component or properly expresses itself in overt behavioral responses. To do so both flies in the face of ordinary experience and impugns those who do genuine good because they "feel" care. But what I do want to suggest is that the psychological interpretation doesn't dig deeply enough and, consequently, misses the full significance of what it means to care. It risks confusing what in fact is a comprehensive offering of one's entire person with a warm, cuddly, and rather cloudy sentimentalism that involves mere emotions. Similarly, it hazards mistaking an integrated way of being that places us in communion with Presence for just a set of learned behavioral responses. In either case, the deep spiritual import of caring is forgotten and our development into full humans is sidetracked.

Caring, then, *genuine* caring, is much more than a psychological phenomenon, although it certainly expresses itself in psychological ways. Instead, it's a repudiation of alienating thinghood and an affirmation of the divine invitation to be, a turning of one's attention to Presence in the world, and a resolve to live in such a way as to progressively become a presence capable of open availability, intimacy, meaning, and creativity. Let's explore more fully what this means.

By now it should be clear that the imitation of divine Presencing to which we're called is always relational. God makes himself present *to* us. It stands to reason that when we follow the divine lead, our presencing is likewise relational: we make ourselves present to something. But it's important to keep in mind that presencing is more than merely a relating-to. More fundamentally, it's also a relating-*for.* God is present to us *for* our sakes. Similarly, when we allow ourselves to be presences, we become present to something for *its* sake. In presencing, then, we make a gift (a "present") of our here-and-now reality, just as God the absolute Presence gives his Reality in the here and now to us.

It's no surprise that our English word *care* is a derivative of *kardia,* the Greek word for heart. For in cultivating presence to and for the sake of something, we give the present of our inmost being: the heart thoughts, the *dialogismoi kardion,* the spirit of the indwelling Word. When we care for another person, for example, we exemplify and project the concern the divine Presence has for all humans. We make ourselves available to that person's needs, her fears, her hopes and joys. We open ourselves up to her wounds and heartaches, not merely for the sake of treating or healing them—although, as we'll see in a later chapter, this is a crucial aspect of caring— but also in order to take them into our heart and share them. In caring for her, we willingly become her keeper or guardian—

not in the sense that we superciliously judge and instruct her, but rather in the sense that we humbly pledge to be present to and for her in her time of travail. And in doing all this, we invite her to discover the deep meaning and promise of her own humanness, to confront the petrification of her alienated heart until she too encounters the Presence who grounds her being. The person who cares presents his heart to another so that the other's heart may open as well. Heart calls to heart, presence elicits presence: such is the creative dynamic of caring.

Another way of putting this is to say that when we are caringly present, we relate in a special heartfelt way. We can better appreciate what's entailed by this kind of heart-relating if we compare it with a mode that, sadly, is more conventional: head-relating.

For too many of us, relating is a standoffish act of intellectual scrutiny. The standard assumption, stretching back at least to Aristotle's day, is that the chief purpose of relating is to acquire knowledge, and that "legitimate" knowledge comes only from impersonal observation and rational analysis. This means that the inquirer ought to cultivate an attitude of clinical detachment when relating to the object of his investigation, warily maintaining distance lest his heart interfere with his head. It need hardly be said that this mode of relating reduces the object of scrutiny to the status of a foreign, other-than-me thing to be pinned on a dissecting board, taken apart, labeled, codified, and appraised. But the head-relater sees this as the merit of his approach. How else can he hope to "know" what the thing objectively is, rather than merely what he subjectively wishes it to be, than by this impersonal mode of relating?

It can't be denied that there's a time and place for head-relating. The cancer researcher probably ought to conduct her laboratory experiments in the spirit of coolly detached objectivity, and the engineer interested in building a dam prudently approaches the problem before him as a puzzle best solved by dispassionate mathematical calculation. Thomas Aquinas calls the relating proper to cases like this *cognoscere per cognitionem,* a head-relating by way of rational cogitation. This kind of relating, abstract, logical, analytical, and nonintuitive, is entirely appropriate when it comes to understanding foreign or alien objects such as cancer cells and trigonomic equations—objects, in short, to which we have no natural affinity or bond.

But *cognoscere per cognitionem* isn't the only game in town. It may be proper for the oncologist or engineer to adopt an impersonally conceptual attitude to malignant cells or mathematical formulae, but such an approach is quite out of place when it comes to relating to cancer victims and villagers whose lives will be impacted for good or ill by what goes on at the lab or construction site. Patients and villagers aren't foreign or alien objects. Rather, they're persons, just like the oncologist and the engineer. There's a deep linkage between the involved parties that immediately makes their relationship different from the one between a human and a mere thing. That bond, of course, is their shared humanness. Consequently, a mode of relating that views patients or villagers as anything less than full-fledged persons is perniciously inappropriate. Instead, St. Thomas says, the proper kind of relating here is *cognoscere per connaturalitatem,* a heart-relating by way of affinity or kinship.

When I relate from the heart, I intuitively recognize in the other something that is intimately my own and hence irresistibly worthy of my deepest personal concern. There's no possibility of detached observation here. Analytical dissection is completely beside the point. What takes precedence is a here-and-now empathic reaching out toward the other, an embracing of him in all his complicated and sometimes messy concreteness, a self-emptying in his direction which, at the same time, is a self-giving. By relating to him in this way, I come to know him as a palpably *real* individual, not simply an abstract datum plugged into a lifelessly theoretical model. I desire his well-being as fervently as I desire my own, because I know him to be a person just like me, possessing the same anxieties and worries, the same hopes and promise, that alternately bedevil and sustain me. He is my neighbor, my kinsman: blood of my blood, flesh of my flesh, spirit of my spirit. His heart is indissolubly linked to my heart, his interests blended with mine, by virtue of the connatural bound that connects us. My sense of meaning and purposefulness is mysteriously bound up with his. When I gaze upon his face, I see my own.[13]

Caring is a *cognoscere per connaturalitatem,* an intimate presencing in the likeness of divine Presencing that demands my whole person, not just my intellect; calls for committed engagement, not distant observation; and provides an opportunity now, in the present, for enhanced meaning and creative flourishing on the part of that to which I present myself. But when I relate in this way with the heart, something else happens as well: I make myself present to and for both God and my own deepest, truest core. The divine Presence that grounds me grounds everyone else as well. This is the connatural link that makes heart-relating possible. So when I caringly open *out* to another, I simultaneously reach *up* to the God that sustains us both, and *inward* to touch base with the Word that dwells in the cavern of my own heart. Presencing, then, is never a one-dimensional relationship. Rather, every act of caring is horizontal *and* vertical, outward *and* inward. When two hearts relate in mutual care, a third heart—God's—is always present (cf. Matthew 18:20). Authentic caring, unlike detached head-relating, is a communal affair.

But the great and mysterious community of heart that

emerges when we care goes even deeper than this. In caringly presenting the gift of my heart to another person, I also give her the divine Heart, the Presence that dwells in me and which is identical to the Presence in her. In laying bare my inmost thoughts, I also call forth identical inmost thoughts that abide in her. In every genuine act of caring, God is the agent and I the conduit. God gives himself through my self-giving; God presences in and through my presencing. And God responds through the other when she reciprocates the care I offer her. All three of us—God, myself, and the other—are connaturally bound by virtue of God's gracious indwelling of the heart. To be caringly present to and for one is to be caringly present to and for all. Once again, caring is communal.

This brings to light a startlingly new dimension to Simeon's insight that the only thing capable of cutting through the alienated heart is the *rhomphaia* of God's Word. Simeon's point still holds. But our discovery of the connatural bond between God and humans now reveals that we're called to be holy words that manifest the Holy Word, to be truth-awakening swords forged from the same stuff as the one Sword. When we embrace our own humanness, we take on the awesome responsibility of giving voice to the Word, supplying the Word with human limbs, human senses, human intelligence—human *hearts*—so that it may present itself to the world. Just as we are liberated by the Word, so we are commissioned to aid the Word in its liberation of others.

Three Stages of Caring

Mary's uncanny encounter with Simeon gives us the secret to holy caring. Old Simeon's riddle is a great gift because it tells us that to become fully human—and hence saintly—we must become presences, as God is Presence. The Greek word for "presence" is *parousia,* a term typically used by theologians to describe the promised Second Coming of Christ that will inaugurate the kingdom of heaven once and for all. But another meaning of *parousia* is "arrival" or "completion." When we become caring presences, when we allow the divine qualities of availability, intimacy, meaning, and creativity to shine through us, we've "arrived." We've reached the point, to invoke Gerald Vann again, where we discern and cooperate with God's Presence "in all things, all situations, all moments, all interests and desires." Our journey is over, our course run, our destiny fulfilled.

But we've still got a long way to go before we get to where we ought to be. Our path to full humanness must lead us into an ever deeper appreciation of the connatural communion between our own heart, the hearts of others, and the Heart of God. Consequently, our journey is divided into three stages. The first is learning to be present to and for the *self.* Until we do this, we're unable to care for *others.* The second stage is learning to be present to and for our *fellow humans.* Until we do this, we're unable to care for *God.* And when, at last, we reach the point where we're able to be present to and for God, we'll discover that our end was in our beginning all along. For as Simeon the cagey Zen master knew, caring for ourselves and for others is all the while caring for God as well. How could it be otherwise in a universe held together by Holy Presence?

2

CARING FOR SELF

O Living Orb of Sight!
Thou which with me art, yet Me!

—Thomas Traherene

ATTENDING TO *COR*

It may seem strange to begin our journey to sainthood by focusing on the self. Self-care evokes the specters of narcissism and egoism, and even those who don't consider themselves particularly religious find something faintly contemptible about such attitudes. Traditional Christian spirituality elevates secular wariness of self-preoccupation into an outright prohibition. (John Calvin, for example, was fond of referring to it as a "pestilence.") The self is viewed as the enemy within whose incessant clamoring and arrogant demands for gratification distract us from God. Jesus taught that anyone who hasn't died to self cannot enter the kingdom of heaven (see John 12:24–25); Paul thanked God that his self had been replaced by Christ (see Romans 6:1–11); and the early desert fathers and mothers took to the wilderness in the hope that its merciless sun would burn away the last vestiges of self. So if we hope to become progressively attuned to the divine Presence in our heart, it seems wrong-minded to deflect our attention by caring for the self.

Well, yes and no. Everything hinges on clearing away the confusion that typically surrounds our concepts of self.

When we do so, a couple of things come to light. The first is that what we normally consider the self is anything but our real identity. On the contrary, it actually prevents us from discerning our underlying true self. To confuse the two is, indeed, pestilential, because it breeds the alienating fall away from humanness into thinghood we touched on in the previous chapter. But to discriminate between them in order to care for and nurture the true self is entirely appropriate. In fact, it's a spiritual necessity, for we'll never be able to embrace the divine gift of being until we become present to and for our true self.

The second point to keep in mind is this: it's impossible for us to be a presence to and for others, either fellow humans or God, if we aren't first present to and for ourselves. Another way of putting this is simply to say that if we don't care for that part of us most worthy of care, we won't know how to properly respond to what's most worthy of care in others, either. The connatural link that binds all hearts together is an enduring reality, woven into the very fabric of existence. But we can become aware of it, and hence enter into our destiny as holy presences, only if we learn to attend to the true self. We oughn't to deceive ourselves, however. This is an extremely difficult undertaking, because the temptation to bypass the true self by focusing on its sham substitute is always strong.

We'll explore this temptation in some detail shortly. But by way of introduction, it's worth observing here that one of the reasons we're so easily confused about who we really are is that we've lost touch with the deep significance of ordinary language. Great truths about both our nature and our destiny are embedded in the words we casually toss back and forth in commonplace conversation. Our forgetfulness of these truths is tragic, because it encourages us merely to dabble our toes in existence rather than diving deeply to discover its secrets. One of the words whose significance has been all but lost is the one we're most concerned with in this chapter: *self*.

When most of us think of the self, what we typically have in mind is "personality": that cluster of moods, attitudes, dispositional habits, and private perceptions, judgments, memories, aversions, and appetites that makes us the unique individuals we are. Because personality—the "me"—is what distinguishes our existence from other people's and gives a sense of *personal* identity, we naturally fall into the assumption that it's also our *essential* identity. We believe it's what we *really* are.

The me is partly hardwired and partly learned. Intelligence levels and temperamental predispositions, for example, appear to be part of the psychobiological package we're born with, while the specific ways they pan out are haphazardly influenced by historical and environmental accidents. Nonetheless, we like to think that the me endures over time, that it somehow always remains intact regardless of how many external changes our bodies and external situations undergo. The psychological advantage of this belief is obvious: durability of the me provides us with a sense of solid grounding in an otherwise unpredictable world. It gives us something to hang our hats on.

But, in fact, the me is rather like a weathercock, blown in any number of psychological directions during a lifetime. Self-images shift with the passage of time, as do interests, values, perceptions of the world and other people, fears and ambitions, motivations and inhibitions. We frequently look back on the me of bygone years and can scarcely believe it once defined who we were. Far from being the stable nugget that enduringly determines identity, the me is a relatively fluid construct extremely sensitive to changes in the climate. It may not be merely the flimsy "bundle of perceptions" that the philosopher David Hume famously claimed, but neither is it the reliably steady-state entity we typically fancy it to be.[1]

My intention here isn't to disparage the me. We are, after all, concretely enfleshed and uniquely tempered creatures who have to deal with a sometimes bewildering environment, and our sense of personal identity is one of the ways by which we cope. Its importance is obvious when we pause to consider that if the me too rapidly unravels (in, for example, psychosis), we lose our bearings in quite horrible ways. The me is an inseparable part of who we are, and to deny this is to slide into an etherial gnosticism that foolishly tries to sever us from our physical and psychological environments. But what I do wish to claim is that the me isn't the sum total, or even the most important aspect, of who we really are. That we believe otherwise is an indication of our deep forgetfulness of what the word "self" actually designates.

So: What *is* the meaning of "self"?

In chapter 1, while exploring Simeon's riddle, we observed that the ancient Greeks used the word "heart" or *kardia* to refer to the part of a human that's most vitally real—the "core" or "center" of a person that constitutes her essence, her true being, what she actually is. This usage carried over into Latin: someone's *cor* or "heart" (linked to the Greek *kardia*) was likewise thought of as her "core" or "center." Moreover (yet another significant connection), the *cor* was reckoned as that part of a person that enables her to exercise *cura*, or "care."

Now, all this is anything but an arcane exercise in etymology. Rather, it's an attempt to bring to surface the deep significance of what we ought to mean by "self," and keeping it in mind will help us get past our confused belief that the me is the final word on identity. Properly speaking, "self" is the unchanging heart or core within us that constitutes our humanness. The *true* self, then, is not the mercurial me. Rather, it's *cor*, and *cor*, not the me, is the proper focus of our care. When we attend to *cor* by becoming present to and for it, we steadily liberate ourselves from the restless me, progress in self-insight, and approximate ever closer to the being to which we're called. We redirect our concern from the me to the *cor*, because we recognize it as that part of us most holy, most worthy of care.

SPIRITUAL HYPOCHONDRIA

When a person takes her center of gravity to be the me, she falls into a pattern of false caring that prevents her from being present to and for *cor*. This pattern comes across to others as egoism.

Popular opinion holds that an egoist is someone with a hyper-inflated esteem of her own talents, strengths, or attractiveness, an infuriatingly cocky and demanding individual who takes as her obvious birthright the duty of others to admire her and cater to her wishes. Most of us can tolerate such self-centeredness only so long before we explode. "You think too highly of yourself!" we shout in exasperation. "You care too much for yourself!"

But the truth is that the egoist's real problem isn't too high a self-regard. Rather, she thinks too little of herself. Her cockiness is a sham and her arrogance a defense mechanism, because her belief that the "me" constitutes her true identity is misguided. When she scrutinizes the me—and she inevitably does, because egoists tend to be obsessively introspective— all its blemishes and blotches come to the fore: vainglorious ambitions, irrational prejudices, aching woundedness, fragile convictions, manic irresolution. After a while, the overall impression she's left with is that the me is hideously diseased.

So the egoist is perpetually beset with nagging anxieties about the state of her me. She feels herself teetering on the brink of disaster, and her overwrought nerves blow up every psychic ache and pain into a life-threatening illness. She tirelessly checks and rechecks the conflicting desires and moods that tidal-wave through the restless me, but the same dismal diagnosis comes up each time. In her own eyes, she's a hopeless case, irremediably blighted by corruption, tossed hither and yon by the fever of conflicting passions and the chills of melancholy and despair.

Far from being arrogantly confident, then, the egoist, in fact, is tormented by a crushing sense of impotence and inescapable doom. This unrelenting burden does, indeed, cause her to be peevishly demanding, but her behavior is grounded in despair rather than hubris. She insists on being the center of attention not so much because she thinks she's better than the rest of us and hence deserves extraordinary treatment, but because she's desperately frightened and cries out for pity and comfort and help. She irritatingly fixates on her own needs and desires because she sees herself as an invalid who must make special efforts just to keep her head above water. What appears to be garden-variety selfishness is actually desperate overcompensation on the part of someone who thinks not too highly of her self, but too little. Her misplaced "care" for the "self"—the me—is really debilitating worry.

This chronic state of worriment over the health of her me is both a reflection and a perpetuation of her forgetfulness of her real identity. Obsessive preoccupation with the me leaves her no time or energy to be present to *cor*. She suffers from a hardened heart that keeps her out of touch with her center. Some part of her dimly recognizes the internal fracture. But as her panicky fear escalates and her self-esteem plummets, she becomes less and less able to correctly diagnose the problem. Instead of realizing that her aches and pains belong only to the peripheral me rather than to the core of who she is, she despairingly writes herself off as a terminal case.

The irony, of course, is that nothing's wrong with her real self, *cor,* and probably not as much amiss with her me as she fears. *Cor* remains healthily intact, untouched by the shenanigans of the me. Moreover, the nature of the me *is* to fluctuate, to hop from one mood or thought or desire to the next in response to an ever changing environment. This is what it does. So the egoist's fear that something's essentially wrong with her is a delusion born from confusion over who she really is. What's broken is her relationship to her true self. She's shut herself off from the center of her being and consequently perverts the care that properly belongs to *cor* to neurotic preoccupation with the me.

What this means is that the egoist suffers from a malady we may call "spiritual hypochondria." She delusionally suspects herself to be mortally ill, and the more she auscultates her interior—the me she mistakes for her true identity—the more she worries over her condition. The self-absorption that comes across to others as galloping hubris is but the outward manifestation of this despairing sense of doom.

To appreciate spiritual hypochondria more fully, let's turn to one of the most chilling case studies of it ever recorded: the unsettling memoirs of the anti-hero in Dostoevsky's novel *Notes from Underground.*

The novel pretends to be the autobiography of someone who describes himself as an "underground man," a person dwelling in shadow and dankness rather than sunlight and warmth. The underground man is a middle-aged civil servant who lives in a squalid and gloomy tenement building of St. Petersburg. Dostoevsky obviously intends his character's external environment as a symbol of his interior state: physical dilapidation outside, spiritual disintegration inside.

From first to last, the thread that holds the underground man's rambling memoir together is unremitting me-absorption. As he himself acknowledges, he suffers from the "full-fledged disease" of "overly acute consciousness,"[2] an obsessive preoccupation with the restless me that inhibits openness to *cor*. Appropriately enough, he begins his story in the first person singular; this self-referential overture sets the tone for everything else that follows. From the very start, the anxious me-absorption symptomatic of spiritual hypochondria is apparent.

> I am a sick man. . . . I am a spiteful man. I am a
> most unpleasant man. I think my liver is diseased.
> Then again, I don't know a thing about my ill-
> ness; I'm not even sure what hurts.[3]

The immediately striking thing about the underground man's opening description of himself is its bizarre fusion of self-fascination and self-loathing, defiant bravado, and pathetic despair. Here, clearly, is someone obsessed with plumbing his darkest depths, even though what he finds there—spite, unpleasantness—horrifies him. Just as obvious is the underground man's conflicted response to his discovery. He throws his ugly self-diagnosis into the reader's face, relishing our discomfort, belligerently daring us to judge him. But at the same time he can't conceal the fact that he's already tried and condemned himself as a repulsive monstrosity.

The underground man's description of himself as "spiteful" is especially revealing. The Russian adjective he uses, *zloi*, carries a number of meanings. In addition to spite, it can connote anger, frustration, malice, and resentment. The underground man is intensely angry, as all frightened persons are, and the eruptions of this anger come across to acquaintances and colleagues as selfish malice and arrogant frustration. Later on he tries desperately to convince himself (and the reader) that the source of his rage is the outside world: the stupidity of his boss, the boring nature of his work, the unfairness of an existence that's never cut him a break. But, in fact, the anger originates from within, spawned by a profound but terrifying apprehension that some internal brokenness prevents him from tapping into a goodness he vaguely senses stirring in his depths. "A great many elements in me" are at war, he says, some proclaiming holiness, others crying hopeless corruption. "I felt how they swarmed inside me, these contradictory elements. I knew that they had been swarming inside me my whole life, and were begging to be let out."[4]

Typical of the hypochondriacal "invalid," however, the underground man protests that he can do nothing to ameliorate his sorry state. He feels he's reached the point of no return, lost the possibility of redemption, and he self-pityingly resents that missed opportunity and suffers cruelly from the frustration it causes. So he hardens his heart against those "elements" within him that suggest a holy center, refusing out of obstinate self-hatred to take their message seriously. "I wouldn't let them out," he tells us. "I wouldn't, I deliberately wouldn't let them out."[5] One catches an echo in this tormented cry of St. Paul's plaintive confession two thousand years earlier that his own awareness of holiness in his "inmost self" was threatened by a formidable army of bewilderingly hostile drives. "Wretched man that I am!" he moaned. "Who will deliver me from this body of death?" (Romans 7:24).

The underground man's dark self-portrait discloses three key characteristics of his plight in particular and spiritual hypochondria in general. The first should come as no surprise after the previous chapter's discussion of spiritual alienation: a person estranged from his *cor* is in bondage. Recall Isaac of Stella's claim that God created us so that we might *be*. For a person to be, he must recognize and embrace all the possibilities of his humanness, and the first step is becoming caringly present to his true self. But a spiritual hypochondriac turns his back on these possibilities by convincing himself that his identity is nothing more than the scattered me he so loathes. In doing so, he imprisons himself in a state of arrested spiritual development. The underground in which Dostoevsky's unhappy memoirist lives is really a dungeon of his own making.

The second characteristic is a corollary of the first. When the spiritual hypochondriac closes himself off from *cor* and sees himself only as a me, he in effect redefines himself as something totally contrary to his true nature: a one-dimensional thing or object that cannot transcend facticity. Objects simply are what they are. They have no real possibilities, because they lack the freedom necessary to go beyond their present condition. They are inescapably at the beck and call of their environment. The only difference between a physical object and a human one is that the environment that enslaves the latter is internal.

The underground man's hopeless conviction that he's unable to escape the push and pull of his me environment darkly illustrates the spiritual hypochondriac's fall into thinghood. As we've already seen, he simply sees no way out: "I am a sick man." Elsewhere in the memoir, he explicitly laments his perceived thinghood when he describes himself as nothing more than an object in a world of objects indifferently ruled by ironclad natural laws. These laws, he says, encase him in stone walls—an image that invites immediate comparison to the hardened heart—and he dismally insists that no effort on his part can break through them. The "conclusions of natural science and mathematics" hold him in a steel grip. Resistance is useless.

> As soon as they prove to you, for example, that it's from a monkey you're descended, there's no reason to make faces; just accept it as it is. . . . [T]here's nothing more to do, since two times two is a fact of mathematics. Just you try to object![6]

"Two times two is a fact": such is the fatalism of the spiritual hypochondriac who reduces himself to nothing more than a thing inexorably dominated by forces beyond his control. All that he is, all he ever will be, is an invalid beset by a hospital chart of incurable woes. This, he concludes, is his essence, his true identity, and his ultimate destiny. No possibilities lie before him other than the ones he now endures. And to be futureless in this way is to lose humanness and take on the passivity of a thing: something that is acted upon but never acts on its own accord, something that can be no other than what it is.

Yet, as I've already noted, a futureless thing is precisely what a human is not and cannot be. Stunted in *cor*-awareness though the spiritual hypochondriac is, *cor* nonetheless endures, and this guarantees that faint echoes of his deep human possibilities occasionally reach him. But instead of seeing them as light at the end of the tunnel, he repudiates them. This move only ratchets up the chronic frustration born from the tension between his confused image of himself as an unsalvageably corrupted *me* and the stirrings of his true self. At the same time the underground man bitterly concludes that the laws of nature entail that "not only couldn't one change, one simply couldn't do anything at all," he quirkily protests: "Good Lord, what do I care about the laws of nature and arithmetic . . . ? I dislike the fact that two times two makes four . . . [N]or will I reconcile myself to it just because I'm faced with such a stone wall."[7]

This irrational back-and-forth movement between fatalism and rebellion reveals a third and startling characteristic of spiritual hypochondria: even though the person alienated from his *cor* desperately wants liberation, he also desperately *fears* it. The spiritual hypochondriac knows himself to be in bondage, and he vaguely senses, as does the underground man, "contradictory elements" of holiness within him that suggest a way out of his misery. Yet the embrace of these elements is a terrifying prospect. He fears that doing so will propel him into an unaccustomed way of being that requires a heartfelt rather than perversely "spiteful" confession of his failure to live up to his human potential, as well as a steadfast resolve to open himself up to his own deepest center. This, of course, means that his self-image, as nothing more than a me, has to be jettisoned. But from the spiritual hypochondriac's perspective, this is a nightmarish fall into nothingness. How could he possibly think otherwise, when the only self he acknowledges is the me? Better to cling with might and main to the me he despises than to sink into the void of its absence. Far better to continue as a hopeless case than to lose personal identity. Even a stunted, blighted life is better than death.

Obviously this is self-deception. Letting go of the me doesn't suck us into the vacuum of nonbeing but, rather, releases us to enter into the life for which we were created. But the spiritual hypochondriac's mistaken belief that the me is his only lifeline paints him into a corner that, in his eyes, allows only two options: cling to his wretchedness or die. As fearsome as the former prospect is, it's infinitely preferable to the latter.

We can see from all this that the root cause of spiritual hypochondria is radical estrangement from *cor*. This estrangement plunges the hypochondriac into despair—which is more than just a psychological feeling of hopelessness. More fundamentally, as the underground man shows us, it's a rejection of hope, a refusal to embrace with trust and gratitude the divine invitation to *be*. That's why traditional theology sees despair as sinful: it's a willful act of rebellion. Obviously not all cases of alienated despair are as acute as the underground man's. Far more likely, as Henry David Thoreau observed, is a state of "quiet desperation" in which we vaguely sense our brokenness but can't muster the courage to face it for what it is.[8] We cover our eyes and stop our ears to the call of *cor* and, in doing so, refuse to be present to and for our true self. When it comes right down to it, the despairing spiritual hypochondriac couldn't care less for *cor,* because he misguidedly cares too much for the me. He hasn't taken to heart T. S. Eliot's plea for the gift of discernment: "Teach us to care and not to care."

DECISIVE MOMENTS

We've already noted one irony of spiritual hypochondria: the individual who sees himself as nothing more than an enslaved me both wants and fears freedom. This leads to a second irony at least as striking as the first: if the hypochondriac is to be liberated from his self-imposed bondage, he must be forced out of it. Neither rational persuasion nor earnest imploring will do the trick. The jolt that takes the spiritual hypochondriac where he longs but dreads to go—straight into *cor*—has to be so coercively strong that it sweeps away all resistance.

That he must be forced into freedom really oughtn't to surprise us. Experience in the everyday world testifies that often we begin to live freely only when circumstances beyond our control—the untimely death of a parent, the loss of a job, or, more affirmatively, falling in love—puncture the protective *status quo* into which we've burrowed. Scripture and honest self-reflection tell us that when it comes to spiritual liberation, a metaphorical kick in the seat of the pants is even more necessary. The hardened heart reaches a point of paralysis where it simply can't whip up the resolve to crack its own casing. So the initiative must be made on its behalf. This is the great insight behind Simeon's image of the sword in the heart.

The internal swordthrust of the ever present Word is the shock that liberates us from our hypochondriacal fixation on the me and releases us to become present to and for *cor*. Sometimes the *rhomphaia* slices through the hardened heart with breathtaking suddenness: Moses before the burning bush, Paul's vision on the road to Damascus. Typically, however, it cuts more slowly and its effects are cumulative rather than instantaneous. When the heart carapace finally weakens and splits, the resulting experience of change may feel dramatically explosive. But, in fact, what's occurred is the final stage in a long process of behind-the-scenes activity in which the "contradictory elements" we all along sensed within us at last break through and overpower our resistance. How could they not? We are beings slated for holiness, not closed-off and futureless objects, and the inmost heart-truth about our real identity must out. When it does, we're set free, as John says (see John 8:32). For some of us, the emancipation may take a lifetime (or even longer). For others, who haven't hardened their hearts to the extent the underground man has, a shorter time may be all that's required for the sword to do its work. But in either case, the freedom to grow into saintliness is our destiny, and God is patient.

Karl Rahner calls the moment in which the divine sword/Word finally breaks through the hardened heart a "decisive" one.[9] A decisive moment occurs when God's living Presence ruptures our complacent existence and provides us with an opportunity—a *kairos,* as the gospelists call it—for insight into who we are. These *kairos* opportunities are "decisive" in two senses.

In the first place, a *kairos* moment is decisive because it brings about a *significant change* in our self-image. It sweeps away our distorted understanding of who we are, allowing us to recognize that our identity is not at all exhaustively defined by the me. The me remains an important and vital part of who we are. As we saw earlier, it provides us with a sense of personal identity, makes us the unique individuals we are, and concretely grounds us in the world. But when the decisive moment of *kairos* liberates us from our fixation on it, we come to appreciate its proper role: to serve as the conduit through which *cor* expresses itself. True, the me will continue to be afflicted in one way or another by a sense of inadequacy, conflicting passions, and bewilderingly hodge-podge associations. But the divine sword reveals the truth that its stormy nature is ultimately subordinate to *cor,* and that the more we attend to *cor,* the more settled the me's restless waters grow.

The second reason the *kairos* moment is decisive is because it forces us to *make a decision:* either to open up to the freedom of *cor,* or to flee it out of a perverse and timid attachment to the me. The sword awakens us to our human possibilities by giving us the gift of authentic self-recognition. But as with all gifts, it's up to us to choose whether we'll accept or decline. This isn't to say that the Word withdraws after the decisive moment, leaving us to stand or fall on our own. Rather, the Presence that percolates throughout reality is always there and never ceases its coaxing. But it's also the case that we must decide for or against it, and this means taking an active role in our growth into humanness after the swordthrust reveals who we are. To passively sit back in the false expectation that God will lead us by the nose toward our destiny as humans and saints is a lapse into the self-imposed thinghood of spiritual hypochondria. So God's rapier slash through the heart lays bare the options and demands a responsive decision. As Simeon said, the Word leads either to the rising or falling of many: rising to humanness or falling back into despairing bondage.

SPIRITUAL NOBILITY

Once we accept the Word's invitation to open ourselves to *cor,* we're on our way to that attunement to the true self that enables us to care for it deeply and authentically. Meister Eckhart, the great and good fourteenth-century Dominican preacher and mystic, can help us better understand the nature of self as well as what it means to be present to and for it.

Eckhart takes as his starting point Jesus' story of "a nobleman [who] went into a far country to receive a kingdom" (Luke 19:12). This parable, says Eckhart, is really about the "outer man" and the "inner man"—what I've been referring to in this chapter as the me and the true self. This is how Eckhart describes the two.

> To the outer man there belongs everything which, while it adheres to the soul, is nevertheless enclosed by flesh and mixed up with it . . . All this Scripture calls the old, the earthly, the outer, the hostile or the slavish man. . . . The other person in us is the inner man, which Scripture calls the new,

the heavenly, the young, the noble man, or the friend. [The inner man] is the field in which God sows his image and likeness and in which he plants the good seed, which is the root of all wisdom, all skills, all virtues and all goodness: the seed of the divine nature. And the seed of divine nature is God's Son, God's Word.[10]

For Eckhart, an authentic human existence involves a gradual moving away from the alienated bondage of the outer man toward the liberating authenticity of the inner one. The outer man is a slave ordered about by destructively "hostile" whims and fears and ambitions. (It's instructive to note that Eckhart's "hostile" whims are very much like the "spitefulness" of Dostoevsky's underground man.) If we throw our lot in with the outer man, we forgo the possibility of humanness and mutate into passive things. But the nobly born inner man is unruffled by the push and pull of baser drives. He is that calm landscape within that grounds "all wisdom, all skills, all virtues and all goodness." The inner man acknowledges the outer man's existence, as the steady mountain acknowledges the blustering wind, but refuses to be moved by him. The relationship between the two, in fact, is just the converse. The outer man bends, or at least ought to bend, to the inner.

According to Eckhart, then, the parable's point is that all of us are nobly born, even if few of us fully realize it. The true self—the inner man—is a "friend," not the enemy the spiritual hypochondriac takes him for, and what we're called to do in this life is to travel single-mindedly in search of our deep nobility or holiness. This is the "divine" end, the "kingdom" to which "we can come through grace" if we but keep to the pilgrim's road with steadfastness and trust.[11]

Good enough. But what, more precisely, *is* the aristocratic inner man that constitutes our true identity?

The clearing: The twentieth-century philosopher Martin Heidegger referred to the self as a "clearing" in the tangled "forest" of existence.[12] He intended many things by this image, but one in particular helps us start to make sense of Eckhart's nobly born inner man.

Imagine yourself thrashing through an overgrown forest. Brambles and saplings are so thick that they cover the ground; you can barely find a way around them. The larger and more ancient trees—oaks, beeches, hemlocks, chestnuts—block out sun and sky with their heavy canopy. Muffled cries of strange birds and beasts echo around you. Everything is covered in shadow, the air is thick and close, and visibility is poor. There's no possibility of getting your bearings. The forest hems you in to such an extent that the only thing you can do is stumble forward, bone-weary, scraped and scratched, and hope you're not wandering in circles.

Now imagine that you crash through an especially stubborn clump of undergrowth and suddenly step out into a clearing. In an instant everything changes. You walk into the center of the clearing and look around. The dark forest encircles you with its ominous foliage, but inside the open space is sunlight and a refreshing breeze. You see the blue, cloudless sky above; underneath your feet is a welcoming carpet of green grass. You can breathe once again. What's more, the unexpected clearing in the forest provides you with a vantage point by which to orient yourself. You stand there, getting a better feel for the lay of the land and the direction you ought to go when you finally plunge back into the trees. But that can wait. For now, all you want is to lift your face to the sky and open yourself to the light and air and silence.

If we think of this open space in an outer, physical forest as an analogy of our interior landscape, we can see what Heidegger is driving at when he says that the self is a "clearing." Each of us struggles through the murky and threatening shadows of the me, sometimes becoming so entangled in its brambles and briars and massive trees that we lose sight of the ground and the sky. We become disoriented because we can't find a vantage point by which to step back from the confusion long enough to see where we are or where we ought to be going. We soon realize that we're lost and, before long, may even come to the heart-sinking conclusion that we'll never find our way out, that we'll remain trapped in the forest forever. This, of course, is the dismal conclusion to which the spiritual hypochondriac comes.

But we do have one thing going for us, even though we may not be explicitly aware of it: the machete of Simeon's *rhomphaia*. Divine grace hacks a path through the forest until we stumble across an open space secreted away in the overgrown me. This is the true self, the nobly born inner man. This clearing is virgin ground, utterly unblemished by the forest. When we stand in it, the silent breeze blows through our hair and we touch the sky. We now have the perspective to see the forest for what it is, as well as to discern that the space we've discovered is our true home, where we ought to be. The clearing is that opening in us that remains always untouched by the great forest, forever uncluttered by its shadows and thorns, and so provides us with the breathing space to cease struggling and become completely receptive—completely *present*—to who and what we are.

What Heidegger calls the "clearing," Eckhart refers to as the "core of the soul." This core, he tells us:

> . . . by nature . . . is sensitive to nothing but the divine Being, unmediated. Here God enters the soul with all he has and not in part. He enters the soul through its core and nothing may touch that core

except God himself. . . . In that core is the central
silence [that allows] the utterance of God's word.[13]

For those of us who identify ourselves with the buzz-
ing and bustling me, this is an astounding passage. What
Eckhart offers us here is a description of self as pure receptivity, that deep core of the soul that is alert or "sensitive" to the
divine Presence. This *cor* is profoundly silent, undisturbed and,
indeed, oblivious to the frantic comings and goings of the
me, because all its energy is focused on attending to Presence.
Since nothing interferes with its concentration, its attunement
to God is unhindered or "unmediated" by the preoccupations
of the me. The entangled forest of passions, ideas, fears,
ambitions, drives, habits, and attitudes that make up the me
surround it, but in itself the *cor* is a tranquil and serene clearing that provides the soul a vantage point by which to
hear—silently, wordlessly, nonconceptually—the silently
wordless Word. It is the uncluttered ground that connects us
with the source of our being, a quiveringly alert availability,
or "active repose," as Maximos the Confessor aptly called it,[14]
that enables us to harken to the still, small voice of God.

Because this *cor* "has nothing in common with anything
else" in our ordinarily noisy and constantly changing internal environment, it is a perpetual "Now."[15] The winds of time
rustle the leaves of the forest, but in the clearing there is only
the stillness of eternity. The noble self, Eckhart tells us, is:

. . . unconscious of yesterday or the day before,
and of tomorrow and the day after, for in eternity
there is no yesterday nor any tomorrow, but only
Now, as it was a thousand years ago and as it will
be a thousand years hence, and is at this moment,
and as it will be after death.[16]

Cor is permanently in the present, and as such is the place where Presence, likewise forever Now-ed, reveals itself.

Finally, the noble man that constitutes our true self is unimpeded freedom, limited neither by me distractions nor the changing warp and woof of time. As a consequence, it isn't clinically definable in the way personality traits and types can be classified and categorized. Being boundless, it is "neither 'this' or 'that.'" It cannot be adequately spoken. Yet for all that:

> [I]t is something higher than this or that, as the sky is higher than the earth. . . . It is free of all names and unconscious of any kinds of forms. It is at once pure and free, as God himself is, and like him is perfect unity and uniformity, so that there is no possible way to spy it out [i.e., to conceptualize and speak it].[17]

By now it should be clear why Eckhart says the *cor* of the soul is the place within us that is "sensitive to the divine Being, unmediated." The reason is that *cor* is that clearing in our being most like God—alertly available, silently attentive, unscattered in "this-es" and "thats," eternally now-ed, boundless—and hence that part of us most receptive to God. There is a connatural affinity (recall our discussion in the previous chapter) between the noble self and the ultimately Noble Self that links them together in "unity and uniformity" and enables them to immediately recognize one another as kindred. And because God is absolute Reality, *cor,* reflecting as it does the characteristics of God, is the part of us that is most real. This doesn't imply that the me of personal identity is unreal or illusory. But it does mean that the me isn't our *true* identity; it isn't that which, at the end of the day, grounds who and what we are. In Eckhart's words, "the inmost core of the soul" is where "human nature takes root."[18] When all is said and done, the me is the forest, the rim, the periphery, that rings but cannot encroach on the open space of *cor*.

Dwelling: Heidegger says that we can live as authentic human beings only if we "dwell" in the clearing of the true self after we've discovered it. To dwell is not merely to squat for a while on an unsettled bit of land or in an empty building, but to put down roots in a permanent home. Anything short of dwelling is a forlornly alienated "homelessness" such as that endured by the underground man.[19]

Eckhart shares this intuition. Our "true life," he says, "is in the soul's inmost recess," and if we fail to comprehend that, it's because we "are not at home there."[20] Coming home, learning to dwell, is a process of growing ever more aware of *cor*, and that means becoming increasingly present to and for it. We dwell when we care for *cor*.

Fortunately, we're never completely lost, even though we often mistake our bearings. Glimmerings of our true dwelling place—those holy "elements" that "contradict" the underground man's baser drives and fears—break through the dense forest. Beneath the hurly-burly of the me, we vaguely sense the stillpoint that is our spiritual center of gravity. When these flashes come to us, we know they're signals from that part of us that is most real and, in spite of our hypochondriacal fears, we can't help but respond with longing. As St. Augustine put it:

> I am aware of something in myself, like a light dancing before my soul, and if it could be brought out with perfect steadiness, it would surely be life eternal. It hides, and then again, it shows. . . . But since it shows itself and draws [my] attention, it must want to allure [me] and make [me] follow it.[21]

These glimmerings are the kairetic moments that force from us the decision either to open up or close down to *cor.* If we take the latter route, we remain homeless. But if we take the former, we begin to dwell and, in dwelling, to care for the self. The key to this is what Eckhart calls *Abgescheidenheit:* detaching one's attention from the clamor of the outer man and single-mindedly turning to the silent receptivity of the inner, noble one. The point is not to destroy the me, but to patiently harness its various faculties—the thoughts, sensations, emotions, and so on that Eckhart refers to as "agents of the soul"—in the service of *cor.* We retain our personal identities— how could we not and still remain the individuals we are?— but now they're suborned to and draw clarity and direction from the eternally now-ed clearing of the true self.

> It is the aim of all God does that the agents of the soul should be re-directed inward, toward himself . . . [B]ut if the soul is scattered among its agents and spread out in externalities, the agent of sight in the eyes, of hearing in the ears, of taste in the tongue, then its inward action is feebler because scattered forces do not fulfill [their mission]. Therefore if the inward work of the soul is to be efficient, it must recall its agents and gather them in from their dispersion to one inward effort.[22]

This in-gathering of the me's scattered faculties accomplishes two things. First, it quiets them down so that we may become progressively attentive to the pregnant silence of the inner self. "When all the agents of the soul are withdrawn from action, then [God's] word is spoken. . . . The more you can withdraw the agents of your soul and forget things and the ideas you have received hitherto, the nearer you are to hearing this word." Second, in quieting the agents of the soul, the in-gathering baptizes them, as it were, with the chrism of *cor*. "The light at the core of the soul . . . spills out, radiates through the soul's agents, passing [to] the outer man. . . . The light in the soul's core overflows into the body, which becomes radiant with it."[23] *Cor* "diffuses" itself throughout the me without diminishing in any way, and the alienated rupture between the inner and the outer man is healed.[24] What was broken is now made whole. Our entire being is ennobled by making contact with that which is most noble within us. We become dwellers, at home in and with ourselves, instead of frustrated strangers in a strange land.

Notice what this in-gathering means. Rather than hypochondriacally focusing on the peripheral me, consciousness makes itself available to the real self in a truly intimate way. Instead of wallowing in a state of self-hatred and impotent spitefulness, our newly recovered availability to who we are at the very deepest level awakens an abiding sense of calm and tranquil meaning. Such is the necessary outcome whenever we touch base with reality rather than delusion. And as we'll discover in the next two chapters, we are now freed from the deadening despair of spiritual alienation to act in the world in a fruitfully creative way—to comport ourselves as authentic humans, not underground men—not "things."

SELF-CARE AND COURAGE

When we attune to the great inner clearing of *cor*, and when we then learn to see *cor* rather than the me as our true center of gravity—our home, our dwelling place—we simultaneously *recognize* our true self *as* a presence and *make* ourselves present *to* and *for* it. We recognize that our deep identity is an unbounded receptivity always available to us, and that it's also the source of meaning and creativity: a presence that reflects and makes room for the divine Presence. In the process, our hitherto dispersed and self-absorbed me opens to the call of the true self and rechannels its energies for the sake of the true self. It makes itself present to and for *cor*. The first brings self-insight, the second freedom to be a human.

As we saw in chapter 1, this presencing is precisely the essence of caring. When we know ourselves to be presences and make ourselves alertly present to who we truly are, we necessarily care for the self. For to recognize that one *is* presence at the deepest core is also to recognize that this presence, connaturally connected as it is to the holy God, partakes of God's holiness. And holiness is a quality to be honored, esteemed, nurtured, protected, celebrated—in short, cared for—because it carries with it the promised gift of being.

The realization of our own holiness gifts us with something else as well: the courageous self-assurance that springs from an awareness that we're destined for humanness and sainthood. Alienation in general and spiritual hypochondria in particular are born from fear and insecurity. Take the sorry example of the underground man, frozen with horror by his condition. Despite his occasional inklings of nobility, he succumbs to the fear that he's nothing more than an impotent thing, flotsam tossed hither and yon by the chaos of his internal environment on the one hand and the indifferent laws of physical nature on the other. His anxiety is so paralyzing that he's even willing to endure his misery rather than risk opening himself to the presence he truly is. Frightened of the hospital list of imaginary spiritual ills contrived by his hypochondria, yet at the same time terrified to venture out of the terminal ward long enough to discover and assent to *cor,* he remains in the dreadful subterranean twilight of suspended existence, neither fully human nor fully thing.

But when we come to recognize the holy presences we are, all that changes. We now know ourselves as unbreakably connected to Being, and this assurance, born of gratitude and peace rather than arrogant defensiveness, gives us the courage to be. We can affirm ourselves, in the words of Paul Tillich, because we know ourselves to be affirmed.[25] The sign of that affirmation is the Godlike clearing within us that constitutes our true identity. We know ourselves to be worthy of care because we resemble he who is most worthy of care, and there is no more solid foundation than this. The courage born of this insight is well expressed by the contemporary theologian Josef Pieper.

> [O]ur acceptance of our own being, our assent to ourselves, our feeling at home in existence . . . this very courage for being is ultimately justifiable only by reference to the initial act of the Creator, who brought us into existence as a reality that henceforth can never be removed from the world, that is not susceptible to "annihilation," and who with absolute finality has declared it "good" that we exist.[26]

We are good, we are noble: this is the sustaining conviction that seizes us when we become caringly present to and for our true self. It is this assurance that gives us the courage to accept the gift of being and enter into the path of conscious holiness.

The first of the *dialogismoi kardion* or heart-thoughts revealed by the sword/Word, then, is that the self is holy and eminently worthy of our care. It's but a short step from this insight to the grateful affirmation that *all* selves are holy and thus equally worthy of care. Each and every person carries nobility within his or her breast, because each is made in the likeness of God and participates, as do we, in God's nobility.

So when we begin to care for ourselves, we cannot help but care for others as well. This is the second stage of holy caring, the second of the *dialogismoi kardion* revealed by God's sword. And it's the subject of our next chapter.

3

CARING FOR OTHERS

Contact with human creatures is given us through a sense of presence.

— Simone Weil

AWAKENING TO KARA

One of the more disturbing signs of our times is the negative spin we tend to put on the word *care*. We gripe about "family cares" and "money cares," complain that we're "careworn" by the pressures of life, and hanker for a more "carefree" existence. Moreover, when we think of a professional "caregiver"—the child-minder, long-term health-care provider, or retirement-home aide—what comes to mind for many of us is a person locked into a drab job that demands long hours but gives back little pay and even less glamour. We're thankful there are people out there willing to take on the task of caregiving, but we're even more grateful that we're not one of them. We've got enough "cares" of our own.

When we use the word *care* in this way, we define it as an unpleasant and unwanted burden that gets in the way of our enjoyment of life. Cares are worries that hassle us, problems that demand too much of our time and energy, roadblocks that deflect us from getting where we want to go. In a similar vein, a generally caring attitude for other persons is viewed as setting us up for grief, frustration, and anxiety unless we know where to draw the line. A little care is okay, even admirable—but a smart person doesn't go overboard. She has her own burdens. Why shoulder someone else's as well? "You've got to look out for Number One," we caution her. "You can't take on the worries of the world! Your problem is that you care too much!" (As if it were possible to care *too* much.)

Now, it can hardly be denied that one of the conventional meanings of *care* is, indeed, "burden" or "anxiety." Even Jesus intended this sense when he advised his disciples to follow the example of the birds of the air and cease their careworn fidgeting about the morrow (see Matthew 6:25–34). Nor would any honest person disagree with the claim that caring is frequently unpleasant. To care well demands that we put ourselves out for another, more often than not at the cost of our own wishes. Finally, it seems reasonable that a person can't and shouldn't "caringly" take on the burdens of the world. Human shoulders simply aren't built for that kind of weight, and to ignore this is not only imprudent, but suggests a certain arrogance.

We can concede these points without falling into the cynical trap of viewing all caring as an unwelcome expenditure of energy if we keep in mind our call to be presences. Caring for another person is perceived as an unnecessary hassle only when we succumb to the me absorption of spiritual hypochondria. The person who thinks of herself as a hopelessly terminal case tends to project, viewing others as she sees herself. So why bother with them? They're imprisoned within their own unbreakable walls, and hence no more salvageable than she. Even if they weren't, the hypochondriac has no time to care for them. She's too preoccupied with stewing over her own list of psychic ailments to think about the well-being of others. If she temporarily breaks out of her me absorption, it's only to demand pity from others or spitefully rail against their very existence. Either way, they are mere things in her eyes: malleable objects to use in the first case, threatening objects to keep at a distance in the second.

But when the *rhomphaia* slices through our alienation to reveal *cor*, we realize, as noted at the end of chapter 1, that the same stillpoint from which we derive our innate nobility lies in the heart of everyone else as well. There are, indeed, mere things in the world, but other humans are no more members of that mute kingdom than we ourselves are. Instead, they, too, are holy presences, sacred clearings in the forest and, as such, are connaturally bound to us. Their hearts call to our hearts, and we long to be caringly present to and for them, even though we're perfectly aware that doing so often means putting ourselves out for them.

In the previous chapter, we saw that confusion over the meaning of "self" was an impediment to genuine self-care, and that the first step toward clarity was rediscovering the hidden significance of commonplace language. Similarly, we can begin to liberate ourselves from misguided cynicism about caring for others if we once again look for the deep meaning embedded in words. In this case, that meaning is supplied by the forgotten Gothic word *kara*.

As with *cor*, *kara* is etymologically derived from *kardia*, or "heart"—in fact, the linkage is even more obvious here. *Cor* is the seat of a person's identity, the defining foundation of who she is, her center, her "core," and to become present to it is to achieve self-insight. *Kara* is the heart-movement we experience when our newly discovered care for self allows us to caringly reach out to others in the world. *Kara* means "grief," "sorrow," "trouble." To care is to grieve. When we open our hearts to our fellow men and women, when we make ourselves present to and for them, we invite them to share their sorrows and troubles with us. This willing receptivity to the wounds of others—or what in English we call "compassion"— is to care for them. *Cor* is the clearing that makes room for *kara*.

But compassionate suffering isn't the entire picture. Otherwise, caring for others would be the horrible burden the cynic believes it is. In making ourselves present to and for others, we live in accordance with our being, with what we are, and this brings a sense of fulfillment that more than offsets the "burdens" of entering into another's pain. Moreover, opening our heart to another through *kara* creatively enables him to responsively open his own heart and thereby begin to live in accord with his own being as well. For the caregiver, this enabling of another's presence is a holy deed that cannot but bring happiness. Finally, presencing to another doesn't at all mean that we share only his wounds. We also partake in the joy of his newfound strength, and this, too, is a source of great fulfillment. From the perspective of a hardened heart, the claim that true joy can come from *kara* is absurd. But for the person on her way to becoming a full human, suffering with another person always carries with it the mysterious promise of meaning and intimacy.

None of this is to trivialize the very real hardships involved in caring for others, but it does remind us that those hardships are laden with the possibility of something quite wonderful. For true joy isn't achieved by closing oneself off to others and living underground. Rather, it comes only from being so compassionately present to and for them that we willingly invite them to share our dwelling place, and this means embracing their darkness along with their light.

SAMARITROPHIA

Before we can explore more closely the nature of caring for others, we need to get clear about why so many of us shut ourselves off from compassionate *kara*. It should come as no surprise that the root cause of the refusal to care for others is spiritual alienation, or estrangement. We saw in chapter 2 that we become alienated from *cor* when we see ourselves as one-dimensional me things. If we refuse the possibility of relating to others in the spirit of *kara,* we do so because we've performed a similar move on them. We turn them into "its," and an "it" is beyond the scope of compassion because an "it," by definition, is incapable of suffering. In short, a person who rejects *kara* alienates himself from other humans by denying them their humanness. This mode of estrangement is the spiritual illness of *samaritrophia*. Samaritrophia is not identical to spiritual hypochondria, but the two share a family resemblance. Both are modes of alienation: from the true self on the one hand, from our fellow humans on the other.

Kurt Vonnegut coined the term in *God Bless You, Mr. Rosewater,* a very funny novel with a deadly serious message. Samaritrophia is a malady "virtually as common among 'healthy' Americans as noses," and is defined as a "suppression" of conscience.

> "You must all take instructions from me!" the conscience shrieks . . . The other [mental] processes try it for a while, note that the conscience is unappeased, that it continues to shriek, and they note, too, that the outside world has not been even microscopically improved by the unselfish acts the conscience has demanded.[1]

As we'll see shortly, the fact that samaritrophia sets in after the conscience has unsuccessfully tried to set the world right is of the utmost importance. The frustration that over-comes a person when her "unselfish acts" fail to lead to spectacular results gives rise to a rebellion of the "mental pro-cesses" that earlier tried to toe conscience's line.

> They pitch the tyrannous conscience down an oubliette, weld shut the manhole cover of that dark dungeon. They can hear the conscience no more. In the sweet silence, the mental processes look about for a new leader, and the leader most prompt to appear whenever the conscience is stilled, Enlightened Self-interest, *does* appear. Enlightened Self-interest gives them a flag, which they adore on sight. It is essentially the black and white Jolly Roger, with these words written beneath the skull and crossbones, "The hell with you, Jack, I've got mine!"[2]

Vonnegut obviously derives the name of his malady from Jesus' parable of the Good Samaritan (see Luke 10:25–37). The Samaritan is an individual who makes himself present to and for the robbed, beaten, and deserted man on the Jerusalem-Jericho road. He cares for the man because his recognition of the connatural bond between them opens him up to the man's suffering. This awareness of connaturality—what Vonnegut calls "conscience"—prompts the Samaritan to go out of his way for the man: binding his wounds, taking him to an inn, paying for his care, promising to return to continue the nurs-ing. He doesn't think twice about this act of "mercy," as Jesus calls it, because he knows that the victim is his "neighbor"—flesh of his flesh, blood of his blood, *cor* of his *cor.*

The Good Samaritan is thus a living example of *kara,* or what (following Vonnegut's lead) we may call "samaritanism." He cares because he is attuned to his own inner nobility, and this in turn allows him to recognize the same nobility in other men and women, even those who lie broken by the wayside.

He sees them as humans, as presences whose being is inextricably linked to his own despite any surface differences in nationality, religion, economic or social standing, and personality traits.

But the "samaritrophian," or the person suffering from samaritrophia, has allowed her ability to recognize and feel care for the presence of others to atrophy. Her alienated self-absorption has buried awareness of the connatural link between her and her fellow humans beneath crushing tons of indifference if not outright hostility. The consequence is that she shuts herself off from others, just as she's already shut herself off from recognition of her own nobility. The damage this hard-heartedness inflicts is twofold: the suffering of others she might've succored goes unaided while, at the same time, her self-destructive refusal to be a human presence wedges her even tighter into isolated and unfulfilling alienation. As Vonnegut sardonically notes, in blocking "the underground rivers that connect her to the Atlantic, Pacific, and Indian Oceans," she foolishly remains "content with being a splash pool three feet across, four inches deep, chlorinated, and painted blue."[3]

Samaritrophia's disintegration of the ability to feel compassion for the wounds of others concretely expresses itself in two related symptoms: "crowding" and "teacupping." Let's examine each in turn.

Crowding: In one of his most haunting short pieces, Thomas Merton suggests that our ethos is "the time of the Crowd."[4] The center of focus has shifted from individuals in all their particularity and promise to statistically anonymous masses. We are more comfortable with "humanity" in the abstract than with concrete "humans." The impersonal crowd has upstaged singular persons.

One needn't look far to find the reason for this shift. We live in an increasingly fast-paced and bewilderingly complex world. The computer revolution may have shrunk the globe but, in the process, has hemorrhaged so much information that we find ourselves unable to keep abreast unless we spin the data into manageable generalities. So we concentrate on demographic curves, vectors of influence, statistical flow charts, bio-medical profiles, and economic projections and, in the process, a firsthand acquaintance with the concrete persons whose lives supply the raw material for the generalizations gets lost. Persons are swallowed by the categories into which we plug them.

Perhaps this kind of "crowding"—a submersion of the individual into statistically nameless and faceless groups—is necessary, at least to a certain extent, in the social and medical sciences. Researchers calculating rates of economic inflation or tracking the probable course of an epidemic need the "big" picture, and concentrating too much on particular trees can blind them to the lay of the forest. As we saw in chapter 1, there's a time and place for the "objective" approach of what Thomas Aquinas calls *cognoscere per cognitionem*. But what may be an appropriate mode of relating when it comes to the special situation of research is pernicious when it trickles over to influence the way we interact with individuals in nonresearch settings—in the "real" world, as it were. Merton's claim is that this is precisely what's happened. More and more, we tend to see the persons who surround us as anonymous members of the great crowd of "billions," "massed together, marshalled, numbered, marched here and there."[5]

What this means, of course, is that we transform living, breathing, aching, and rejoicing subjects into impersonal objects, things (so far as we're concerned) to be defined and classified by external traits and functions. The high school kid behind the fast-food counter or the middle-aged mechanic who inspects our car becomes a faceless member of the "service" crowd. Folks in other countries or other states or even just across the county line become nameless statistics in the "foreign" crowd. People who hold religious or political or ethical convictions different from our own are relegated to the anonymity of "ideological" crowds. The physician we go to when we're ill is defined by the medical diplomas hanging from her office wall, the professor who teaches us is just the number of books she's published, the senator who represents us is nothing more than her congressional voting record. Our crowding surrounds us with unambiguous robots, each with a function to perform and a role to play as defined by the category he or she belongs to. We haven't the interest or leisure to know anything more about them than this. The time of the crowd is also the time of "no room": no room for the messiness of genuine engagement. No room for heart-relating, no room for presence.[6]

Most of us, at one time or another and to one degree or another, fall into the habit of crowding. Fortunately, we usually catch ourselves before we go too far; our conscience warns us that we've overstepped the line. But the samaritrophian has imprisoned her conscience in a dark oubliette and, as a consequence, her crowding has become second nature. Wherever she looks, she sees only things. Her landscape is dotted with nothing but one-dimensional objects that occasionally arise from the gray mass to perform certain functions and then unobtrusively sink back into its anonymity once they've finished their assigned task. She resides in a kingdom of its, and its conveniently call for no care on her part. Indeed, it would be the height of irrationality to suppose that they could. One doesn't feel compassion for a broken TV set or an auto that's run its last mile. The appropriate response is to reach down into the available crowd of televisions and cars and pull up new ones. Granted, some models are better than others—but any one will do in a pinch, because when push comes to shove, there's not much difference between them.

Teacupping: This brings us to the second characteristic of samaritrophia. Crowding is the method by which the samaritrophian transforms persons into objects. Teacupping, or the response Vonnegut sacrastically dubs "Enlightened Self-interest," is the way she treats them after they're transformed.

The word *teacupping* is adapted from the following passage by Henri Nouwen:

> When you take a teacup by its handle, you can keep it at a distance and look at it from all sides. You can make it an obedient instrument in your hands. You can manipulate it in any direction you want. You have complete control over it, for it is in your hands, your power. Many of our human relations are of this order.[7]

For the samaritrophian, *all* human relations are of this order. Her crowding surrounds her with anonymous objects and, as we've seen, the value of an object—fast-food kids and physicians no less than televisions and automobiles—is defined solely in terms of its use. So the samaritrophian hoists the Jolly Roger and sails the seven seas in search of plunder, looking for objects she can manipulate or "teacup" for her own ends. In her eyes, humans become utensils or tools to be used and discarded at will. Like any other object, they're entirely disposable. If a teacup's handle breaks, throw it away and find a new one. True, the teacup may have been a highly prized, fine piece of china. But caring *about* the value of an object is entirely different from caring *for* a person. The first is a detached appreciation, the second a committed engagement.

Teacupping, like all forms of piracy, is concerned with seizure, control, and possession. The primary objective is to exact obedience from the object being manipulated, to force it to bend to one's will and service one's desires. Nouwen notes that sometimes the seizure is a physical bullying, such as when we're mad at a child and "take him by his ear and shake his head like a teacup." But generally our power plays are more subtle, and hence more effective, than this. "Worse than these physical forms is the mental form in which we can take our fellow man. We can take him by his vulnerable spot, his hidden weakness, and make him an object at which we can look from a distance, which we can turn around and lead to the place we want it to go."[8]

For example, we manipulate those human-objects foolish enough to genuinely care for us by blackmailing them. If they don't act exactly as we wish them to, we inflict punishment by showering disapproval on them. This is their weak point, their "vulnerable spot," and we take full advantage of it when it suits our purposes. Or we gossip about co-workers and public figures, blowing up their weaknesses into damning rumors, exerting our power over them by damaging or destroying their reputation. Or we insinuate that human-objects reeling from poverty or social injustice have brought misfortune on themselves through their own stupidity or character flaws. In these and a thousand other ways, we maraud through the Kingdom of Its on a rampage of conquest and control. We need have no compunction about doing so; after all, others are only objects to be used. It's not as if we owed them anything. Besides, it's in our best interest—our "Enlightened Self-interest"—to teacup. The more objects we own and manipulate, the wealthier and more untouchable we are. And isn't that what life's all about? I've got mine, Jack. To hell with you.

On the surface, the samaritrophian appears to be a callously muscle-flexing lout, an utterly self-serving egoist who forces people into the inert status of things only to use and abuse them, an individual so crazed with the lust for power and dominion that she doesn't have a decent heart-stirring in her body.

But we need to be careful about making a hasty judgment here. We saw in our exploration of spiritual hypochondria that what seemed blatant egoism in fact was deep-seated fear and insecurity: the underground man comes across as an insufferable megalomaniac because he cares too little rather than too much for himself. Something similar underlies the spiritual disease of samaritrophia. Crowding and teacupping are desperate power plays motivated not by a coldly indifferent absence of compassion, but by a sickeningly wounded sense of the suffering of others. This isn't to deny that some individuals simply seem to be born without conscience and enjoy manipulating others, but the samaritophian isn't one of them. Her problem isn't that she doesn't care for others. Rather, it's that she cares unwisely.

The merit of Vonnegut's description is his recognition of this fact. Samaritrophia, he tells us, attacks those individuals "who reach biological maturity still loving and wanting to help their fellow man."[9] But as the years roll by and they sense their earnest efforts haven't improved the "outside world" a single bit, they begin to suspect, first despairingly and then cynically, that humans are irredeemable. Something must be so broken in the human soul that it's simply unfixable. So the incipient samaritrophian's view of others undergoes a shift. She begins to see them as inescapably enslaved by inner demons whom she's powerless to vanquish, and her disap-pointed weariness soon persuades her that caring for such creatures is not only futile but stupidly self-destructive. It only drains her own resources. Why would any sane person con-tinue butting her head against an immovable brick wall? Why set oneself up for nothing but pain?

So her conscience—her caring, her presencing—begins to shut down in self-defense. The process is typically incre-mental rather than sudden. She removes herself gradually from the heartache of caring for others—first this one, then that one—until before she fully grasps what's happened, she's crowded everyone around her into the status of faceless, anonymous things. It's but a short step from this withdrawal from engagement with others to samaritrophia's full-blown symptom of teacupping. After all, the proper response to things is to use them for one's own end.

The spiritual burnout that Vonnegut calls samaritrophia is not fanciful fiction. All of us have felt it to one degree or another in different periods of our lives, and it's an ever threat-ening occupational hazard for professional caregivers. In the language of psychotherapy, it's called "secondary stress syn-drome" or "vicarious traumatization." A professional counselor begins to slide into the syndrome when the plight of her patients so overwhelms her that she experiences "feelings of numbness, avoidance patterns, intrusive thoughts and images or . . . physical reactions." She finds herself growing increas-ingly "cynical and suspicious of others' motives," feels "vulnerable or helpless," and experiences "a feeling of alien-ation from others or even . . . a general disorientation."[10] Her empathic connection with suffering others, as well as her sink-ing conviction that her care for them is little more than cut-and-paste triage, saps her energy as well as her sensitivity. Persons seeking her help lose their particularity, their concreteness, and blend into the anonymous crowd of "patients."

The burned-out counselor, like anyone suffering from samaritrophia, crowds and teacups, not because she never cared but because she failed to care wisely. "Teach us to care and not to care," Eliot prayed: this is the lesson we must take to heart if we wish to navigate our way around samaritrophia and awaken to *kara*. And the key to this discernment is presence.

CHRISTS ON THE SIDEWALK

In one of his rare forays outside Kentucky's Gethsemane monastery, Thomas Merton experienced a moment of insight—a kairetic moment of decisiveness in which the sword turned in his heart—that blasted away the last vestiges of his own samaritrophia. This is how he describes it.

> In Louisville, at the corner of Fourth and Walnut, in the center of the shopping district, I was suddenly overwhelmed with the realization that I loved all those people, that they were mine and I theirs, that we could not be alien to one another even though we were total strangers. It was like waking from a dream of separateness, of spurious self-isolation . . . This sense of liberation from an illusory difference was such a relief and such a joy to me that I almost laughed out loud.[11]

A bustling downtown shopping district isn't exactly the spot most of us envision when we think of spiritual breakthroughs. Our imaginations prefer the more "proper" settings of windswept mountaintops or lonely deserts. Yet when it comes to caring for others, beehives such as city street corners *are* the "proper" setting. For the sidewalks, if we but knew it, are crowded not with impersonal statistics but with hearts that hold within them the silent stillpoint of *cor*. If we know how to look, we don't see ourselves surrounded by mere its. Rather, we see Christs—we see beings radiant with presence. Like Merton, we gaze on them and discern "the secret beauty of their hearts, the depths of their hearts, where neither sin nor desire nor self-knowledge can reach, the core of their reality, the person that each one is in God's eyes."[12]

When this happens, we no longer seek to defensively isolate ourselves from others by crowding and teacupping them. On the contrary, we recognize the holy connaturality that links their hearts to ours—and to God's—and we joyfully cry:

> Thank God, thank God that I am like other men, that I am only a man among others . . . God Himself gloried in becoming a member of the human race. A member of the human race! . . . I have the immense joy of being man, a member of the race in which God Himself became incarnate.[13]

We saw in the last chapter that overcoming selfalienation means diving beyond the me to be present to and for the true self, that permanent and ever now-ed receptivity to God that constitutes our real identity. When we do this, we care for self. Analogously, escaping the snare of alienation from others—for that's what samaritrophia actually is—means looking beyond the surface me of the other, which is just as confused as our own, to be present to and for his *cor*. The spiritual burnout characteristic of samaritrophia comes from focusing exclusively on the other's me. When that's all we see and relate to—when that's all we care about—of course we set ourselves up for the crushing frustration that eventually para-lyzes what Vonnegut calls "conscience."

There are two reasons for this. In the first place, the me in and of itself *is* unsalvageable. We can patiently and gently counsel another's me, nurture it, encourage it, and tend to it until the cows come home, and it will still continue to run its wild and neurotic course. Little wonder, then, that our fixa-tion on it eventually persuades us that "the world hasn't been even microscopically improved" by all our efforts to care. In the second place, when we focus on another's me at the expense of its underlying *cor,* it only stands to reason that we eventually begin to respond to others in terms of crowding and teacupping. The me in and of itself *is* thing-like, totally under the dominion of its whims, fears, freewheeling associa-tions, and imperious emotions. It is unfree, and to be unfree is to be a thing.

To care for the other's me at the exclusion of his *cor* is a foolish caring, an unwise caring. It closes us off from making ourselves present to his real identity and thus appreciating him for the holy human he is. Even worse, it encourages him to think of himself as nothing but a me, thereby preventing him from plumbing his own depths to become present to the holy *cor* he actually is. In caring unwisely, we facilitate spiri-tual hypochondria on the part of the other and samaritrophia in ourselves.

But just as hypochondria is escapable, so is samaritrophia. Like Merton, our hardened hearts can be gra-ciously opened by the sword/Word to reveal the *dialogismoi kardion* embedded within them. We can be present *to* other people as the Christs they are, and be present *for* them, in wise rather than foolish care, in order to help them recognize their own holy Christ-selves. As I said in chapter 1, we can become—indeed, we're called to become—liberating swords in God's hand, living words by and through which divine Presence quickens the desire in others to *be*.

PRESENCING TO CHRIST-SELVES

In the first half of the nineteenth century, Søren Kierkegaard launched an attack against what he called "Christendom"—the too-comfortable perversion he feared Christianity had become in the hands of "churchy" people. With an evangelical fervor as uncompromising as it was sophisticated (and this second characteristic is what distinguishes it, alas, from much of our present day revivalism), he insisted that Christians were out of touch with the living God. Either pentecostal fervor had been lost to a chilly religiosity that emphasized formulaic homage to an other-worldly, aloof Christ, remotely seated on an inaccessible throne; or attunement to the living presence of God had given way to a byzantine ancestor-worship of a far-removed and time-shadowed historical Jesus. In either case, a vitalizing sense of the here-and-now presence of Jesus the Christ had been sacrificed for a lethargic religiosity that pushed God to the outer reaches.

What the properly pious churchgoers of his time had forgotten, claimed Kierkegaard, is that "in relation to the absolute, there is only one time, the present."[14] Christ is not some remote entity we will face only in the distant future when we die. Jesus is not merely a figure who lived in a long-ago and alien past. If God *is*, then God is *now*, just as surely amidst us today as he was two thousand years ago in Israel—and as he will be in the next life. The absolute God-in-Christ is our "contemporary," always present to us, ever discernible in the quotidian rounds of our lives. And since this is the case, "it is easy to see that in relation to him there is only one situation, the situation of contemporaneity; the three, the seven, the fifteen, the seventeen, the eighteen hundred years make no difference at all."[15] A God safely relegated to either the distant past or the distant future is not an "actuality" for us. "Only the contemporary" is actual. Consequently, "whatever true Christians there are in any generation are contemporary with Christ."[16]

What Kierkegaard calls "the situation of contemporaneity" is identical to presencing. We begin to enter into an immediately contemporaneous relationship with Christ when we become caringly present to and for *cor,* the silent heart-depth which, being like God, is totally receptive to God. The eternally now-ed *cor* connaturally attunes us to the here-and-now presence of the eternally now-ed Absolute, and we know that beneath the underlying coming and going of the me lies our permanent dwelling place: the Christ-self. As Merton wrote a hundred years after Kierkegaard, Christ's "image is in us all, and we discover Him by discovering the likeness of His image in one another."[17]

Merton's insight is a good one for, as we've seen, the openness that reveals our own true identity stretches beyond ourselves. Once we're liberated from the fears and insecurities of the me, we recognize that the same ever now-ed Absolute that grounds us abides in others as well. We know full well that the other's me (like our own) seduces him, as Merton says, into many "absurdities," "terrible mistakes," "sorrows," and "stupidities,"[18] and that until his me is properly suborned to *cor,* he'll continue to blunder around as a less-than-human thing. But we also sense the deep self within him that contains the possibility of holiness, and we cannot but be caringly drawn to it.

When we make ourselves present to it, the Christ-self within him unmistakably shines forth in such a vibrantly contemporaneous fashion that there's no longer any danger of closing ourselves off from it and lapsing back into the crowding and teacupping characteristic of samaritrophia. We've focused on the other's true identity, who and what he really is, and the brilliance of that vision transfigures him, and us, and, indeed, the entire world. We've heart-related to the stillpoint in him, discovered that it's also the stillpoint within us, and we celebrate rather than despise his existence. He is, in fact, no longer an "other." Now he is someone with whom we're in communion at the deepest possible level. In Merton's words, recognition of another's true identity is affirmation of "the pure glory of God in us."

> It is so to speak His name written in us . . . It is like a pure diamond, blazing with the invisible light of heaven. It is in everybody, and if we could see it we would see these billions of points of light coming together in the face and blaze of a sun that would make all the darkness and cruelty of life vanish completely.[19]

To see and affirm others as the contemporaneously sparkling Christs they are: this is what it means to become present *to* them. And such presencing is a gift bestowed on us by the sword in the heart.

CREATIVE ATTENTION FOR CHRISTS

Although becoming present to others is crucial, it's not sufficient. Genuine caring is always a double movement: presencing *to* must flow into presencing *for*. When it comes to others, it's not enough to connaturally respond to their *cor* and see them for the Christs they are. We must somehow awaken them to their own true identities, and thus nurture their blossoming forth as humans. We are called, in short, to treat them in such a way as to encourage self-recognition on their part, to be there for them so that they might *be*. After his sidewalk epiphany, Merton realized the urgency of this calling. "If only they could all see themselves as they really are!" he sighed.[20]

The heart-response of *kara* enables us to be present for others. We saw at the beginning of this chapter that the Gothic word *kara*, derived from the Greek *kardion*, is a compassionate suffering with others that also brings great joy and fulfillment. At first glance, this is counterintuitive: How can suffering give rise to happiness? But we can start to make sense of the claim if we take time to consider a mode of relating that the twentieth-century mystic Simone Weil calls "creative attention." When we creatively attend to another, we go out of our way ("attention" is derived from the Latin *tendere*, "to stretch") to extend to that person the joyous gift of being and, in so doing, help that person discover the Christ he or she is.

According to Weil, there are two basic ways we can treat others: with contempt or with attention. If we take the first route, we adopt the attitude of crowding and teacupping. But as we've seen, this is really to treat people as if they're things, denying them the opportunity to be human: "The man who is entirely at the disposal of others does not exist." Our contempt for them reduces others to the miserable status of commodities that are used and then thrown away. We "absent" or kill their "humanity," turning them into "anonymous flesh lying inert by the roadside."[21]

When we take the second route of creatively attending to others, we refocus on their humanity—or their holy *cor*. Years of being treated as things may have convinced them that they really are nothing more than utensils to be manipulated and discarded when no longer serviceable. After all, people tend to see themselves as others see and treat them. So in a tragic way, persons who have been conditioned to think of themselves as mere objects grow blind to their own brilliant potential as Christs. From their stunted vantage point, the *cor* within them simply doesn't exist. The purpose of creatively attending to them is to remind them that it does. Consequently, "creative attention means really giving our attention to what does not exist" in the minds of persons who have not yet awakened to their *cor*. Its goal is to help them shed the layers of thingness imposed on them so that they can touch base with the receptive stillpoint within their hearts—and the only way to do that is to meet them where they are, in their lowliness and suffering. We make ourselves their peers so that we can raise them to a higher level. As Weil notes, "He who treats as equals those who are far below him in strength really makes them a gift of the quality of human being, of which fate had deprived them."[22]

The way in which we do this is to treat them with patient generosity and compassion. In the language of Kierkegaard, we make ourselves contemporaneous with them, acting as a Christ in order to nurture their own self-recognition as Christs. God generously self-emptied in Jesus the Christ to make himself utterly available to fallen humans. He came down to our level that we might be raised to his and find meaning and fulfillment in our lives. Moreover, in making himself our equal—our peer, our contemporary—God compassionately participated in the suffering woundedness to which we're subject, helping us to see the suffering as a means to salvation.

In becoming present for others, then, we replay the two central mysteries of faith: the generous Incarnation on the one hand and the compassionate Passion on the other. We "reproduce," so far as is possible, "the original [incarnational] generosity of the Creator." We reenact, again as best we can, God's self-emptying and voluntary acceptance of suffering in order to "give existence to a being other than" ourselves. "Generosity and compassion are inseparable, and both have their model in God."[23] Together, they constitute the heart-response of *kara*.

In practical terms, the *kara* of creative attention entails that we go out of our way to give whatever we must to breathe self-recognition and rebirth into others. Such a sacrifice requires a voluntary "diminution" of our own interests, a "restraint and renunciation" of our own wishes and desires. We accept "an expenditure of energy, which will not extend [our] own power but will only give existence" to another.[24] All acts of creation, artistic or otherwise, require this profligate outpouring of inner resources: "work of the highest order, true creation, means self-loss."[25] We give, even to the point of exhaustion, to bring forth something valuable. In the case of presencing for others, that which is brought forth is more precious than anything else imaginable.

It's not at all necessary that this energy be spent in undertaking dramatic, world-shaking actions. The sacrifice isn't for the sake of an abstract "humanity," but rather for the concrete person before us who hurts too much to see herself as the brilliant point of light she is. So the generous self-emptying of *kara* is content with simple acts such as holding a sobbing child, listening to the story of a laborer crushed by a lifetime of hard work and heartache, sitting by the bedside of a sick acquaintance, bringing books or cigarettes to a prisoner, taking the time to keep a lonely stranger company, spending a few hours each month chatting with elders at a retirement center, sticking by an angry and frustrated acquaintance even as she lashes us with her rage.

Obviously there will be times when these acts of presencing for others are not just inconvenient but downright burdensome. We may feel as if we're being stretched too thin, that we're being taken advantage of, that we've no time left for ourselves, that we've simply nothing more to give. Our self-emptying will bring us suffering, and then we'll be asked to empty ourselves even of that in order to go on serving others. In our destitution we may well feel as if we have no place of our own to lay our heads. But what we must keep steadily before us is that self-denying suffering for the sake of others is a small price to pay for helping them see that they are worthy of our care, that they're not disposable and contemptible objects, that something beneath all their anguished brokenness shines with goodness and the promise of wholeness, and that we're ready—no, that we're *privileged*—to do whatever we can, by example and deed, to liberate their affirmative self-recognition. We incarnate Christ so that they might become Christs.

The suffering we will endure by creatively attending to others goes beyond even this. "Still more," says Weil, "to desire the existence of the other is to transport [oneself] into him by sympathy, and, as a result, to have a share in the state of inert matter which is his."[26] In diminishing ourselves for the other, in becoming present for him as a contemporaneous equal, we open ourselves in *kara* to the chaotic pushes and pulls of his out-of-control me. The connatural yearning of our *cor* for his *cor* draws us to him just as he is, with all his blemishes, self-destructive urges, and paralyzing fears, and we willingly participate in the anguish of his alienation in order to help him dive beyond it and discover being. We are no longer outsiders looking in. We compassionately enter into his wounded space—come to where *he* is, as Luke (see 10:33) says the Good Samaritan did with the man by the wayside—

give ourselves over to his "inertness," and work from within his pain so that our *kara* can lead him to *cor*. We reenact the Passion, dreading to drink from his cup of bitterness, bleeding on the cross to which he's nailed, sharing in his death-agony, so that in dying with him he may resurrect with Christ.

It's important to note, as Weil does, that our willingness to caringly suffer for a person isn't prompted merely by some kind of high-minded altruism or fidelity to a moral principle. The self-emptying into another's pain required by *kara* simply can't be sustained by either of these abstractions. From a psychological perspective, the affliction we endure in creatively attending to our fellows is too intense to be motivated by just our own will. Any "normal" person would buckle under the strain. From a spiritual perspective, authentic caring isn't possible if our attending to another is "merely regarded as an occasion for doing 'good,'"[27] for then our true focus isn't the concrete individual before us so much as a bloodless ideal. The man or woman we succor becomes only an opportunity for good works and, in the process, is once again relegated, although in a subtle way, to the status of a thing—this time, a thing to be fixed. He or she becomes just a means to an end, with the end here being our own self-promotion as a good or noble or ethical person.

No, genuine *kara* is possible only when there's personal engagement on our part, a living commitment to the flourishing of the person to whom we attend—a deeply-rooted realization, in fact, that she really isn't an "other" so much as an extension of myself, my contemporary. I enter into her woundedness because I empathically recognize that her own tormented yearning to be is my own, that the me-driven confusions that prevent her from coming into her humanness once enshackled my spirit as well. And I recognize all this not because I'm particularly intelligent or sophisticated in the ways of psychology and theology, but because the sword/Word compassionately opened my heart just as I'm now trying to open hers. Just as caring for self is a grace-gift, so is caring for others. God's presencing to and for me empowers me to presence to and for others. God's creative nurturing of me into being gives me the strength to creatively nurture others. I am the sword, but the hand wielding me is God's. In Weil's words:

> God alone has this power, the power really to think into being that which does not exist. Only God, present in us, can really think the human quality into the victims of affliction, can really look at them with a look differing from that we give to things, can listen to their voice as we listen to spoken words. Then they become aware that they have a voice, otherwise they would not have occasion to notice it.[28]

FROM *KARA* TO COMMUNITY

Now we're finally in the position to understand why *kara* is a source of great joy as well as great suffering.

First, joy is experienced by the person to and for whom we make ourselves present. In recognizing her true Christ-self and caringly attending to it, we become conduits for her of the availability, meaning, creativity, and intimacy that forever emanates from divine Presence. When she experiences God's revitalizing Presence through us, her bondage to thinghood is broken. She knows herself for who she really is—*cor*—and can begin the process of suborning the restless me to the "central silence," as Eckhart put it, of the internal Word. She enters into the way of holy being, of full humanness, that for which she was made and that for which she's always yearned in an inarticulate, unaware fashion. Our *kara* brings her the joyful peace of fulfillment. And now that she's able to care for her true self, she's also empowered to extend the gift of care to others as well.

Second, joy is experienced by the person who makes himself present to and for others, for from the Gethsemane and Golgotha of self-emptying *kara* comes the incredibly rewarding happiness of knowing that one has aided God in bringing another person to life. The suffering endured by the caregiver when he stretches himself to the breaking point for another is now seen as birthing pangs. "If anyone is in Christ, he is a new creation; the old has passed away, behold, the new has come. All this is from God, who through Christ reconciled us to himself and [in turn] gave us the ministry of reconciliation" (2 Corinthians 5:17–18). The other is reborn by the caregiver's efforts, brought into the fullness of being, and the caregiver shares in the marvelous wonder of this rebirth. Creativity, as Weil pointed out, demands all from us (as it demands all from God). But when the masterpiece—in this case, a human being—is completed, we see that the travail was worth it all along.

There's yet a third reason why *kara* brings joy: compassionate suffering leads to community, to a spiritual state of *being with humans* in intimate relationships rather than merely *co-existing alongside things*. In making myself present to and for others, I help them become present to and for me as well, and the alienation that ruptured our communion with one another is healed. Fragmentation gives way to wholeness, desolate isolation blossoms into enriching companionship. The divine *rhomphaia* that splits open our hardened hearts clears the ground for reciprocal recognition, respect, and care. We empathize with one another's woundedness, affirm one another's personal identities, and celebrate the *cor* that connaturally links us together. We become the occasions for bringing meaning and intimacy to one another. And in communing with one another in this way, we glimpse the kingdom that is our birthright and our destiny. None of us can fully enter that kingdom unless all of us enter it. But we edge ever nearer to it as we broaden the domain of care and community, and our hearts can't but trill with joyful anticipation at the prospect of finally arriving there.

For the kingdom of heaven is nothing less than that blessed state in which we become fully human by unreservedly accepting the chrism of being and its invitation to make ourselves caringly present to one another as well as to the Presence that binds all hearts together. We belong to one and the same body of Christ (see Romans 12:5), if we but knew it, and our membership in that holy incorporation means that we are Christs indelibly stamped with the signature of Christ. When we reach out in care for one another, we affirm who we are and what we are made for. Even more, we reach out for God, because he is present, as Simone Weil says, "at the point where the eyes of those who give and those who receive meet."[29] Entering more fully into this great mystery, the culminating stage of holy caring, is the subject of our final chapter.

4

CARING FOR GOD

The completely lit light is invisible; that which is
greatly celebrated and many named is ineffable and nameless.
That which is Present in all and discoverable from all
is incomprehensible and inscrutable.

—Dionysius the Areopagite

ATTUNING TO *KHORA*

Meister Eckhart once shocked his congregation by pray-
ing that God would rid him of god.[1] Some five centuries later, Paul Tillich said very much the same thing when he
recommended that if the word *God* offends, throw it out.[2] It
is, after all, but a sound or a scribble on a piece of paper. But
because of the psychological and conceptual baggage it carries, the word is potent. Misconceptions about its meaning as
well as personally distasteful associations clustered around it
can prove to be stumbling blocks. So if the term stands in the
way of making contact with divine Presence, get rid of it. Find
a less offensive word—or no word at all—by which to gesture
at the experience of the Holy. In throwing over god, we free
ourselves to discover God.

This is sage advice. Far too many of us (even theologians and philosophers, who really ought to know better) fall
into the habit of thinking of God as a thing or object, and
thus find ourselves blocked off from Holy Presence by our

ideas about God. Granted, this God-thing is "divine," and hence not quite the same as any ordinary or commonplace object. But the difference is generally sensed as one of degree rather than kind, for we suppose that the Divine-thing, like any other object, can be scrutinized, analyzed, dissected, assigned more or less definite characteristics, classified, and then neatly tucked away in an appropriately labeled file folder.

Sometimes the thinging is quaint: we image God as a bearded geriatric in flowing robes or a moon-eyed youth who lived in Palestine two thousand years ago. Sometimes the thinging is sophisticated: we conceive of God as a spiritual force that permeates the universe (something like a physical law), a metaphysical entity, or the conclusion of a logical syllogism. Usually, however, the thinging is a rather eclectic mishmash of the two: God as a personal metaphysical entity or a loving spiritual force. But the result is the same. God becomes a thing—puzzlingly unconventional, somewhat amorphous, fuzzy around the edges but, for all that, a thing. And then we scurry around trying to describe the Divine-object as accurately as we can. We become observers relating to a God-thing in the detached mode of *cognoscere per cognitionem*.

This tendency to reduce God to an object of scrutiny is on a par with our alienated mutation of the self into a me-thing and our brothers and sisters into crowded and teacupped other-things. It's one of the symptoms of a hardened heart that fearfully refuses to make itself available. But it's not an inevitability, for when the sword/Word opens the heart to reveal the *dialogismoi kardion,* we become aware of a great truth that we've carried within us all along but somehow suppressed along the way: God is the indefinable and mysterious Being that beckons us toward being. God is not a thing to be conceptually observed or imaginatively pictured, but a Presence who is connaturally experienced heart to heart. And that Presence is a paradox: brilliantly immediate yet darkly hidden, contemporaneously personal while at the same time inscrutably transcendent, felt but unspeakable, fantastically intimate but also frighteningly awesome. God's Presence shimmers through each and every created object, yet God himself is no object. God's Presence grounds the existence of things but, in itself, is as far removed from thinghood as day from night.

In earlier chapters we saw that the first step toward genuine caring is unlearning confused ideas about self and others. We discovered that when we harken to our hearts, the *cor* that constitutes our true identity is disclosed, as is the truth that our relationship with other humans is properly founded on *kara.* The same rule applies here. If we hope to care for God, we must disabuse ourselves of our confused thinging of divine Presence—we must throw out god, as Eckhart says, to make room for God. When we do so, what's revealed is that God is best thought of as *Khora.* Holy caring first discloses *cor,* then *kara,* and finally *Khora.* I'm unaware of an obvious etymological linkage between the three. But the homonymous similarity of *Khora* to both *cor* and *kara,* not to mention *kardia* (heart) and *cura* (care), is striking—and, for our purposes, important.

Khora is a Greek word that means "open space." It was sometimes used by ancient Hellenes to refer to a marketplace or pubic square. But behind this rather pedestrian meaning lies one of great significance—commonplace words, remember, often have deep meanings embedded within them. The almost forgotten sense of *Khora* especially intrigued Plato, and we may turn to him for a deeper appreciation of it.

At one point in his dialogue *Timaeus,* Plato discusses three realms of reality. The first is sensible, the order of material objects perceived through the senses. The second is intelligible, the class of concepts knowable by reason. Objects in the first realm change through time, while objects in the second remain "always the same"—a geometrical axiom, for example, isn't subject to the fluctuations of history or fashion in the way that a sensible tree or stick of furniture is.

Common sense usually stops with this twofold division. But Plato intuits another realm of reality, one that can't be straightforwardly perceived or thought yet nonetheless generates and grounds both material and conceptual objects. This "third kind of being, . . . difficult of explanation and dimly seen," he calls *Khora*. Since *Khora* is neither a sensible "this" nor an intellectual "that," it is "incomprehensible," "invisible and formless Being." Yet for all its ineluctability, *Khora* is that which is most real, and it is also that which creatively imparts being and meaning to the other two realms. Plato gets this point across by referring to *Khora* as the "mother" or "nurse." It is the mysteriously fecund "receptacle" or womb from which lesser beings are birthed, and thereby serves as a "home" for "all created things." To invoke the language of an earlier chapter, *Khora* is the supreme clearing in the forest of existence, that open space which provides room for everything else to come forth and flourish. All things that are dwell in that open space, derive their very being from it, and thus reflect it, albeit in a dimly mysterious manner.[3]

What Plato calls *Khora* is divine Presence, that incomprehensible and formless Reality that caringly generates and nurtures the world, makes itself intimately available in and through created things, imparts meaning and significance to their existence, and ceaselessly calls them to itself. It is nothing—literally, a no-thing, a clearing, an empty space—but its very nothingness is what makes it the supremely creative Reality it is. Because it is nothing, it cannot properly be thought of as an object. Doing so distorts the nature of *Khora,* mutating it into just another thing in a world of things. And because it is neither a sensible nor intellectual object, it's beyond perception or thought. *Khora* can be experienced, but the encounter is always ineluctable and mysterious. Intuitive glimpses are vouchsafed when we attune to *cor* or *kara,* but these glimpses are inevitably fleeting. Consequently, our attempts to speak *Khora,* much less to pigeonhole it in some contrived theological or philosophical category, inevitably fall short of the mark. We can gesture at *Khora* through poetry and song, but because it's neither a "this" nor a "that" (and we're reminded here of Eckhart's identical description of the inner "noble man"), it cannot be adequately thought or spoken.

When Eckhart tells us to forsake god in order to find God, and when Tillich recommends that we do well to throw away the conventional word *God* if we find it a stumbling block, they're operating from an intuition of the *Khora*-nothingness of divine Presence. Their advice may be shocking to those of us who think of God as an object, but it's hardly blasphemous. Nor, as we'll discover shortly, is it unbiblical, for Scripture consistently tells us that divine Presence, even when it reveals itself, does so mysteriously. If we would learn to care genuinely for God, we must drop our fidelity to the God-thing and become present to and for the ultimately unknowable *Khora.* In fact, the point can be safely put in even stronger language: caring well and truly for God is always a confession of agnosticism, while misguidedly focusing on God as a thing is in effect a form of atheism. The agnostic cares too much for God to reduce divine Presence to a thing. The atheist cares too little for God to acknowledge and celebrate God as *Khora.*

Habitual Piety

We've already examined two ways in which the hardened heart cuts itself off from the *dialogismoi kardion* embedded within it: spiritual hypochondria on the on hand and samaritrophia on the other. In the first case, we refuse to be present to and for *cor* because we neurotically take our real identity to be nothing more than a hopelessly terminal me-thing. In the second, we refuse to be present to and for our sisters and brothers because we deny them *kara* and thus reduce them to nothing more than anonymous other-things to be used and discarded at will. Either move is symptomatic of the alienation that sets in when we lose touch with the Word eternally indwelling us.

It's but a short step from thinging ourselves and others to thinging God. The heart that finds itself unable to open up to God for the supreme Presence he is suffers from what may be called "habitual piety." As I suggested in the preceding section, this alienation is really an atheism, albeit a disguised and hence especially insidious kind. The person who's fallen into it *thinks* that she's a genuine God-believer. But in fact, she isn't. On the contrary, her misguided transformation of God into an idol-thing is as much a rejection of God as the strident disbelief we conventionally associate with the word *atheism*.

The same Graham Greene who started us on our exploration of holy caring by observing that the proper end of life is sainthood also gives us a clue to why habitual piety is a subtle form of atheism.

> God might forgive cowardice and passion, but was it possible to forgive the habit of piety? . . . [Sinners] could be saved, salvation could strike like

lightning at the evil heart, but the habit of piety excluded everything but the evening prayer and the Guild meeting.[4]

For Greene, *piety* is a code word for an entrenched state of spiritual inertia in which we replace a genuine openness to the living Presence of God with the mechanics of religious observance. The person who totters on the brink of self-destruction because of unchecked passions or moral weaknesses is closer to God than he may imagine. He at least retains the capacity to feel deeply, even if his feelings spiral in undesirable directions, and this generally means he's aware, although perhaps in only an inarticulate way, that something is broken in his relationship with self, others, and God. In Simeon's language, such a person experiences the initially discomfiting thrust of the heart-*rhomphaia* that reveals glimpses of the abyss into which he's fallen. A nagging awareness of one's alienation is the first step to salvation. Jesus came to tend the sick, not the healthy.

But the habitual pietist is untouched by such vexing anxieties. She has repressed her capacity to feel deeply for the sake of a comfortable equilibrium. Everything in her spiritual world is in properly tidy order. She knows the rules and she abides by them, cozily ensconcing herself within the orbit of routine and predictability. God wants her at evensong, and so she faithfully attends. God wants her to join the altar guild, and she becomes a member. God wants her to say her rosary every day, to refrain from intemperate language and bad thoughts, to confess regularly and observe days of obligation and, in general, to live up to all the other rather mild requirements of mechanical piety that regulate her life. She does so scrupulously, and accordingly takes it for granted that her relationship with God is everything it ought to be.

Yet for all her punctilious observance of religious pro-
priety, the habitual pietist is an infidel. In spite of her confident
assertions of belief in God, she is an atheist. For in fixating on
a nitpicking fidelity to the letter of the law, she has forsworn—
or "excluded," as Greene puts it—a relationship to the divine
Presence who always and everywhere transcends the law. The
"god" she worships, a blandly unimaginative schoolmarm
whose only concern is that the rules be followed, has taken
the place of the *mysterium tremendum et fascinans.* Her "god"
is neither mysterious nor awe-inspiring. It evokes no distressing feelings of inadequacy or exhilaration, nor does it aim to.
It wields a prosaic catechism manual and a hymnbook rather
than a flaming sword and, together, they exhaustively answer
every question and resolve all perplexity. It is a thing, a reliably familiar object, a plastic Jesus whose every crease and
fold are precisely in place.

And this means that the habitual pietist in effect is an
unconscious atheist: a person who claims belief in God but,
in fact, disbelieves—or, more precisely, *refuses* to believe,
because she senses at some deep level that the real God, the
God of Presence, the God of unsayable mystery and unthinkable paradox, the no-thing God of *Khora,* is too unsettling to
contemplate. Far better to worship a domesticated plastic Jesus
than face the ferocious sword/Word that will turn her spiritually snug world upside down. Far better to care for a god-thing
than for Presence.

We saw in chapter 1 that alienation is the child of fear
and insecurity. The person suffering from it is so frightened
of what he takes to be a threat to his well-being that he shuts
himself off from any possibility of intrusive disruption. The
spiritual hypochondriac balks at opening himself to *cor*
because he fears that a fall into its silent clearing will damage
the me to which he pins his identity. The samaritrophian

gradually ceases opening in *kara* to others because a few hard knocks have persuaded him that all the caring in the world won't make a microscopic bit of difference.

Similarly, the habitual pietist atheistically closes herself off from Presence because she fears it will shatter her comfortable religiosity (as, indeed, it will). Like the spiritual hypochondriac and the samaritrophian, her problem is not that she doesn't care, but that she cares unwisely. She directs her attention to something unworthy of the care she bestows on it. But this move, like all strategies born of fear, is self-defeating. For in retreating into her pious sanctuary, she alienates herself from the true God, refuses the gift of holy caring, and retards her development as a human.

As I suggested at the beginning of this chapter, the disguises under which the habitual pietist cloaks her atheism may take many forms. One of them, as we've just seen, is a relentless "churchiness." But there are other versions that better suit different temperaments. A person of an intellectual bent excludes Presence from his life by concentrating on an abstractly conceptual god-thing spun from passionless logic and dusty treatises. An individual with aesthetic inclinations may gravitate toward a god-thing of carefully wrought stained glass, gracefully carved mahogany, and theatrical glitter. Others may cling to an all-purpose-tool god-thing, a divine gizmo whose only proper function is to fix situations that go bad. There are any number of substitutes that serve as buffers against Presence, but what they all have in common is their user-friendliness. In adopting them as gods, habitual pietists aim to insulate themselves from the uncanny mystery, the unresolvable bafflement, and the life-changing disruption of an encounter with *Khora*. But they also cut themselves off from the overwhelmingly holy sense of meaning, intimacy, creativity, and freedom that comes only from being caringly present to and for Presence.[5]

Agnostic Courage

In opposition to the fear-inspired habitual piety that drives us into the arms of user-friendly god-things and turns us into unwitting atheists, Scripture uniformly recommends what might be called "agnostic courage." Agnosticism in this context isn't a suspension of belief *that* God is, but rather a humble confession that because God isn't just another knowable object in a universe of objects, we can never presume to exhaustively comprehend *what* God is. As the great systematic theologian Thomas Aquinas conceded, "the human mind . . . does not reach a knowledge of what God is [*quid est*], but only that he is [*an est*]. [There is] an ever growing knowledge of him as distant from everything that appears in his effects."[6] This doesn't mean that God is utterly beyond our ken; divine Presence does reveal itself to us. But none of these revelations—even the ultimate one of the Incarnation—does more than gesture at the mystery of *Khora*. To cite Thomas again, "This is what is ultimate in the human knowledge of God: to know that we do not know."[7]

Consequently, the person who hungers for the Divine must find the courage to admit that the God for whom she searches remains just over the horizon, just out of reach, forever beckoning but irremediably ungraspable by intellect, religious rite, or worded description. She must muster the bravery, in other words, to live with the fact that the Presence she craves is also, in a manner of speaking, Absence. As Simone Weil wisely observed, "Contact with God is given us through the sense of absence." Far from shrinking in horror from this absence, we must allow ourselves to be "rooted" in it.[8]

It's entirely appropriate that the first two commandments in the Hebrew Decalogue warn us against worshiping lesser deities and making "graven images" of God (see Exodus

20:3–4). Both of these lapses, of course, are symptoms of habitual piety. They deny the uncanny ineluctability of God for the sake of tangible god-things utterly devoid of mysterious Presence. The mere fact that they're given pride of place in the Decalogue suggests that scriptural authors were well aware of the urgency with which we thing God if given half a chance.

In contrast to such safely knowable gods, Exodus describes divine Presencing as enshrouded in a "thick darkness" or impenetrable "cloud" (see Exodus 20:21; 24:15). Although Moses' experience of God's self-revelation is unmistakably powerful and life changing, it's also quite unfathomable. Similarly, when God at last responds to Job's tormented questioning, the communication is so incomprehensible that Job gives up trying to understand it, concedes that Presence "hides counsel without knowledge," and accepts the impossibility of understanding God as just another object in reality (see Job 42:2). He bows his head in humility before the divine mystery, and finds the courage to admit he cannot capture Presence in the conventional theological or philosophical concepts offered by his companions. God's ways remain inscrutable. As the Psalmist says, "the knowledge of [God] is too wonderful for us;/I am not empowered to attain it" (139:6).

The insight that Presence cannot possibly be captured in conventional images runs as a subtext throughout the great prophetic denunciations of idolatry. "Truly," cries Isaiah, "thou art a God who hides youself,/O God of Israel, the Savior" (45:15). The Hebrew word translated here as "hides" means "to be absent," "to conceal," and "to keep secret." The implication is that God's hiddenness is not merely the unhappy consequence of shortsightedness on the part of humans, but part and parcel of what God actually is. God isn't playing a coquettish cat-and-mouse game. Instead, God reveals himself in the only way he can: as a cipher.

The same theme is carried through in the New Testament. Even God's most concrete revelation, his incarnation as Jesus of Nazareth, is shrouded in mystery and obscurity. Faith tells us that Jesus is fully human *and* fully divine, but the intellect is stymied by this apparently contradictory marriage of limitation and infinitude, history and eternity, immanence and transcendence. Jesus radiated Presence. Merely to touch the hem of his garment was to sense it (see Mark 5:25–29). But for all his enfleshed, here-and-now tangibility, his very being still baffled even those persons closest to him. John the beloved disciple, whom tradition tells us was closer to Jesus than any of his followers, nonetheless confessed that the truth about Jesus is unknowable by the world (see John 14:17). Indeed, the entire prologue of John's Gospel may be read as an attempt to speak the baffling Presence/Absence of the incarnate God. Paul insists that the Presence of God in Jesus is "unsearchable" and "inscrutable" (see Romans 11:22), his gifts "inexpressible" (see 2 Corinthians 9:15), and the peace he brings beyond understanding (see Philippians 4:7). Indeed, he goes even further: although Jesus is the clearest earthly revelation of God, that revelation is always mysterious because the very act of divine self-emptying underscores God's elusive hiddenness (see Philippians 2:5–7). Yet John and Paul, along with Old Testament authors, see the inscrutability of God as something to be courageously affirmed rather than timidly sidestepped.

Scripture's insight that the living God is ultimately unknowable, and that consequently the most appropriate attitude on the part of a person seeking God is courageous agnosticism, so impressed early Christian thinkers (particularly those in the Greek tradition) that they advocated what became known as "apophatic" spirituality. The apophatic way (from *apo*= "beyond" and *phasis*="image") teaches that divine Presence may be experienced by heart-stirrings, but never comprehended through images or concepts contrived by the head. Because God is not a knowable object, the intellect will never be able to neatly define and name his essence, and any attempt to do so only separates or alienates us from him. Better, then, to let go of our images of the Divine and trustfully—courageously—sink into the unspeakable *Khora*-nothingness which is God. At the very least, we ought to acknowledge that all our words and images about God are symbols that do little more than awkwardly gesture at the truth and, if we're not extremely cautious, actually distract us from Presence.

The first explicit defender of the apophatic way was the anonymous mystic who's come to be known as Dionysius the Areopagite, also called the Pseudo-Dionysius. Writing sometime between the second and the sixth century, Dionysius taught that even though God is the cause of everything that is, he in himself is no-thing or non-being (*anousia*). This characterization is remarkably similar to Plato's intuition about *Khora:* God is the fecund womb that generates the objects that comprise reality, but isn't himself a member of the order of beings, or objects. He is beyond objecthood, radically other than a thing: hence no-thing. As the Areopagite says in the passage quoted at the beginning of this chapter, the divine Nothingness shimmers in and through the created realm, but itself remains "invisible," "ineffable," and "nameless."

Thus for Dionysius, God is that creative mystery which is "obscured to all light and hidden to all knowledge."[9] God is a "darkness beyond light," a "hidden mystical silence" inaccessible to "the senses, the imagination, and the intellect."[10] Referring to the Exodus story that describes Moses' dramatic wilderness encounter with Yahweh, Dionysius reminded his readers that even here direct knowledge of divine Presence was unattainable. Moses immediately experienced Presence, but only in the mode of a:

> mystical
> darkness of unknowing;
> in this he shuts out every knowing apprehension
> and comes to be in the wholly
> imperceptible and invisible.

God's unconcealing to Moses is a "knowing beyond intellect," an unknowing that reveals "nothing."[11] It is the awareness of a Presence that manifests as Absence—absence of describable features, absence of representational images and symbols, absence even of abstract qualities. This Presence is so beyond comprehension that the very words Dionysius himself uses to make his point are inadequate, for Presence is no more "darkness" than "light," no more "nothing" than "something." Presence is:

> not something among what is not,
> not something among what is,
> not known as it is by beings,
> not a knower of beings as they are:
> There is neither [reason], name, or knowledge
> of it.[12]

And, in agreement with Paul, Dionysius cautions us that even when Presence reveals itself in Christ, the revelation is shrouded in darkness.

> It is hidden after the manifestation; or, to speak more divinely, it is hidden *in* the manifestation. For this remains hidden about Jesus: the mystery in him is not brought forward by any logos

[reason] or intellect. Rather, it remains ineffable
in being spoken, and unknown in being thought.[13]

In fourteenth-century England, another anonymous
mystic, the author of the tract entitled *The Cloud of Unknowing,* uses Dionysian-inspired apophatic language to make a
similar point. God, he says, is forever hidden in a "cloud of
unknowing." This cloud can never be penetrated by intellect
or emotion. At best, we can only open our hearts to its mystery in the hope that an occasional flash of lightning will dart
through the cloud and briefly illuminate the murkiness. Even
when this happens, however, the sudden encounter with Presence will afterwards be unspeakable. "I am at a loss to say
more," he confesses, "for the experience is beyond words. Even
if I were able to say more I would not now. For I dare not try
to describe God's grace with my crude and awkward tongue.
In a word, even if I dared I would not."[14]

To a careless reader, these words may come across as
timidity: the author of *The Cloud of Unknowing* doesn't "dare"
speak the experience even if he could. But in truth, the passage illustrates the courage of agnosticism. It takes stalwart
resolve to forbear the temptation to make an encounter with
Presence less uncanny than it is by forcing it into the straightjacket of language and concepts. Humans simply feel
uncomfortable if not outright distressed when confronted with
the divine Mystery, with the supreme Is-Who-Is-Not. We prefer the safe harbor of clearly defined categories to the
unchartable deep of the unspeakable—the *unthinkable*—and
this usually sends us scurrying for the life jackets of conventional words and images.

Such is the trap a habitual pietist falls into. Unable to
face the Presence which is always a *mysterium tremendum et
fascinans,* she latches onto her user-friendly substitutes, the

god-things that are predictably, and hence nonthreateningly, delineated and defined. But the agnostic steels himself to the Presence which is Absence, opens himself to its floodwaters, and lets them take him where they will. He possesses, in short, the courage to abandon himself to the darkness of *Khora,* trusting against all reason that this is his real home. He may not, as the author of *The Cloud of Unknowing* advises, "learn to be at home in this darkness." It will always remain disturbingly uncanny. But he knows that "if in this life you hope to feel and see God as he is in himself, it must be within this darkness and this cloud."[15]

Caring for *Khora*

It's entirely appropriate that the *Cloud*'s author uses the expression "God's grace" to refer to the experience of Presence, for it reminds us that we do not—we cannot—*make* ourselves aware of *Khora.* The alienation of a hardened heart, as we've seen time and again, is a form of spiritual enslavement, and the slave is powerless to strike off her own chains. Self-liberation minimally demands the desire for freedom. But the habitual pietist, just like the spiritual hypochondriac and the samaritrophian, fears any rupture of her perverse *status quo.* Uncomfortable and even unendurable as her bondage may at times be, it's preferable in her mind to the hazards of a fresh start.

So something more than mere willpower is needed to escape pietistic alienation from God—what the *Cloud*'s author calls "grace," and what Simeon refers to as the sword/ Word of God. The *rhomphaia* slices through the carapaced heart to disclose the inmost awareness, with which we're born but timidly repress, that God is *Khora* rather than a user-friendly idol. Just as God's presencing to and for us discloses our true identity as well as the Christ-identity of our sisters and brothers, so God now reveals God. This revelation is one of the decisive moments Karl Rahner writes about. When the truth that God is the supreme Is-Not dawns upon us, we either renounce our god-things and open ourselves in fear and trembling to the Presence which is Absence, or we recoil from the unconcealment and desperately scramble back to the false security of our alienated bondage. But we must choose.

If our decision is *for* Presence, our lives irrevocably change. One is again reminded of the biblical stories of Moses' rebirth before the burning bush and Paul's conversion on the Damascus road. Easy religious slogans, hackneyed ways of defining God, and conventional modes of thinking about the Divine fall by the wayside when the heart accepts the revelation of *Khora*. Dull complacency and the arrogant confidence that one knows all there is to know about God crumble, and in their place emerges a humble confession of ignorance that at the same time is a radical receptivity to Presence. Another way of expressing the transformation is to appeal once again to Thomas Aquinas's distinction between distanced head-relating and the heart-relating of connaturality. The habitual pietist sees her god-thing as an object to which she has merely an external relationship. But the person whose heart has been opened senses a deeply intimate, meaningful, and creative affinity between herself and *Khora* that forever destroys the possibility of aloofly thinging it, and when this happens she moves from atheistic alienation to a genuinely caring relationship with God. She forsakes god for God, and allows herself to become present to and for the unfathomable, inexplicable Presence.

Let's examine more closely what it means to be present to and for God.

Presencing to *God:* It should be clear from what's already been said that becoming caringly present to God entails an openness to the *Khora*-revelation and a courageous acceptance—indeed, affirmation—of God's incomprehensible hiddenness. But this immediately raises two questions: How does one do this? and How is a connaturally meaningful, creative, and intimate relationship possible with such an elusive Presence?

To answer these questions, we may return to *The Cloud of Unknowing.* The secret to becoming present to *Khora,* its author tells us, is a two-step process that cultivates first detachment and then awareness.

Most people, particularly those suffering from full-blown habitual piety, spend colossal amounts of energy trying to clear away or penetrate the unsettling cloud of darkness that envelopes God. As we've seen, there are as many strategies for doing this as there are individual temperaments: conventional churchness, cerebral theologizing, aestheticism, and so on. But what's called for is a relinquishment of these thinging strategies, an intentional submersion of them in yet another cloud, one of "forgetting." "You must fashion a cloud of forgetting beneath you," says the *Cloud*'s author, "between you and every created thing."[16] Even though this will be "toilsome" work, it's a necessary housecleaning for that receptivity to *Khora* which is the final goal.[17]

The "created things" we forget when we sink into this second cloud are all the pietistic ideas and images of God we normally cling to. Theological concepts fall by the wayside, as do both conventional devotions and private prayers. Not that anything is intrinsically wrong with such practices; in and of themselves they're "laudable." But the problem is that we can become so focused on them that they get in the way of an immediate experience of divine Presence. The means we use to struggle toward God can be mistaken for ends. As the *Cloud*'s author worries, "If your mind is cluttered with these concerns, there is no room for God."[18]

> I go so far as to say that it is useless to think you can nourish [a relationship with God] by considering God's attributes, his kindness or his dignity; or by thinking about our Lady, the angels, or the saints; or about the joys of heaven, wonderful as these will be. I believe that this kind of activity is no longer of any use to you.[19]

So his advice is to let them go. Clear them from your mind, especially those most precious to you. Allow them to disappear in the cloud of forgetting. "Say to your thoughts, 'You are powerless to grasp God. Be still.'"[20]

It's important to note that the forgetting recommended by the *Cloud*'s author isn't just a refocusing of attention from the external world to one's interior. Introspective withdrawal into one's mind or imagination isn't a genuine forgetting so much as a mere shift of focus that moves one from the realm of material objects to the realm of mental ones. But because God is not located in any particular place—only objects have spatially discernible position—he is found in neither realm. To look for him there is actually to remove oneself from the possibility of Presence. "When your mind consciously focuses on anything [inner or outer], you are there in that place spiritually, as certainly as your body is located in a definite place right now." So forgetting is not a relocation from an outside place to an interior one, but rather a surrender of *all* place—a "nowhere" or "blind nothing." "Do not try to withdraw into yourself, for to put it simply, I do not want you to be *anywhere;* no, not outside, above, behind, or beside yourself."[21]

What the *Cloud*'s author is recommending, then, is a letting go of all the preconceptions about God by which we normally try to orient ourselves. We must be stripped naked of the distractions that block our receptivity to Presence, detached from our pantheon of user-friendly god-things so that we may finally experience God. Note that this forgetting of our objectified images and concepts about God is quite similar to the *Abgescheidenheit,* or detachment from the me, Eckhart claimed is the necessary condition for discovering *cor* (see chapter 2). It also bears a family resemblance to that purging of our crowding and teacupping tendencies required for a *kara*-recognition of others as contemporaneous Christ-selves (see chapter 3). The spiritual life is nothing if not seamless. *Khora*-care follows the lines already laid out in our explorations of self-care and other-care. The general principle behind all three—*Khora*-care, self-care, and other-care—is that vision is unclear if the eye is blemished. Clear the eye of obstructions, and the happy outcome is farsightedness.

Once we reach the "nowhere" found only in the cloud of forgetting, we're ready to engage in the second movement of being caringly present to *Khora,* what the *Cloud*'s author calls a "naked intent toward God," a "reverent, conscious openness to God."[22] God-things that hitherto blocked our receptivity to the unnameable Presence have been eliminated, the spiritual palate has been cleansed, and we enter into a state of single-minded attentiveness that allows for an experience of the dark brilliance of God. The soul is "continually poised and alert at the highest and most sovereign point of the spirit."[23] Here it stands silently in the midst of the cloud of unknowing, and its silence is an acutely receptive sensitivity to the lightning flashes of Presence that occasionally illuminate the darkness. In achieving that curious marriage of unruffled tranquility and sharp attentiveness the *Cloud*'s author refers to as poised alertness, we make ourselves present to the advent of Presence. We enter the divine clearing.

The "naked intent" advocated by the *Cloud*'s author is really a radical kind of empiricism: we suspend or forget all our preconceptions about God in order to become "openly conscious" of God as he really is. When we do so, we forgo our futile efforts to utter or even conceptualize the experience. Instead, we simply stand before it in unblemished receptivity to what it has to reveal. Because we neither can nor try to filter it through image, concept, or words, it presents itself to us in all its immediate but nonetheless inscrutable reality. In becoming present to the Is-Which-Is-Not, to the Presence that manifests through Absence, to the divine Darkness punctuated by divine Lightning, we touch base in a pure and unmistakable way with the No-Thinged *Khora* that grounds the existence of things.

But this immediately raises the second of our two questions: How can standing with naked intent before *Khora* bring the meaning, intimacy, and creativity that, as we saw in chapter 1, comes with an experience of Presence?

The answer to this question is easy to state—although, cautions the *Cloud*'s author, not easy (or perhaps even possible) to comprehend. We are brought to a condition of spiritual fulfillment when we stand in the "nowhere" of presence to *Khora,* because we've finally arrived where we ought to be. Recall that *parousia,* the Greek word for "presence," also means "arrival." In working our way past our alienated thinging of God and becoming present to the dark mystery he is, the heart-affinity between ourselves as presences and God as Presence—an affinity ruptured by our spiritual hypochondria, samaritophianism, and habitual piety—is reestablished. We arrive at or achieve our destiny. We at last grow into our own as humans made in the *Khora*-image of

God. We become what we were intended to be all along: presences so alertly receptive to the divine Presence that a mysterious interpenetration between us and God occurs. The *Cloud*'s author puts it this way: "You have transcended yourself, becoming almost divine, because you have gained by grace what is impossible to you by nature . . . Almost divine—yes, you and God are so one that you . . . may in a sense truly be called divine."[24]

What sense can we make of this?

Look at it this way. Our true self, *cor,* is made in the image of *Khora*. As we saw in chapter 2, *cor* is the stillpoint of the soul, a quiveringly alert receptivity that provides a clearing in which we can experience the corresponding alert silence of God. Like God, *cor* is neither a temporal "this" nor a spatial "that," and so is utterly beyond worded descriptions or even comprehension. But because *cor* is a reflection of the darkly mysterious yet absolute reality of God, it also carries within its no-thingness the possibility of deep meaning. To care for *cor,* to be present to and for it, is not merely to discover one's true identity. It is also to become aware, even if in only a dim, indirect way, of the absolute reality of God, one radiant with a profound sense of meaning, an intuition of the intimate connection between our mysterious center and his, and a longing to creatively *be* in order to live up to the heart-connection between us.

Moreover, as we saw in chapter 3, our recognition of *cor* also allows us to awaken to the presence of *Khora* in others. We see them not as mere things but as meaningful presences contemporaneous with both ourselves and the absolutely meaningful (but again incomprehensible) Presence that shimmers forth in all humans. We reach out for them in *kara*-care, and in doing so both reflect and reenact the intimacy and sacrificial creativity of God's primordial care for all humans.

We nurture them in the direction of their own discovery of being, toward their own *parousia*. We become the wombs for them that God is for us.

Now, in being caringly present to and for others, and thereby experiencing and expressing meaning, intimacy, and creativity, it's obvious that we were all along making ourselves present to the *Khora* connaturally linked to our soul as well as the souls of our sisters and brothers. We may not quite have been aware of it at the time. We may merely have thought we were growing in self-insight and compassion for others. But, in fact, we were steadily moving toward God and, in the process, reflecting more and more profoundly God's absolute Presence. When we finally come to the point where we courageously cease our thinging of God and stand nakedly before *Khora,* we recognize that the meaning, intimacy, and creativity we earlier encountered and reflected are ultimately grounded in him. We darkly know the true source of the Holiness we glimpsed in ourselves and in others. And in that moment of dark insight, when we encounter in all its breathtaking immediacy the meaningful, intimate, and creative Presence we but dimly intuited before, we arrive at our completion. We are finally so one with God that "we may in a sense truly be called divine."

In becoming present to the unsayable Presence, then, we not only intentionally enter into the "nowhere" of *Khora* that grounds our being in holiness. We also discover that we were there the whole time, had we but known it.

Presencing for *God:* The relationship of caring is never exhausted merely by becoming present *to* that for which we care. Opening up to the spiritual nobility of our true self and recognizing the Christ-selves of others is only half of the equation. Genuine caring also entails becoming present *for* that which we care about. When we make ourselves present for *cor,* we embrace its stillness and allow it to be the center of our identity that it properly is. Similarly, when we reach out in *kara* to others, we become present for them as nurturers of their own self-discovery and growth toward holiness.

Caring for God, likewise, is a twofold movement of presencing *to* and presencing *for.* The author of *The Cloud of Unknowing* has helped us understand what it means to caringly open up *to* divine Presence. Now it's time to consider what it means to be present *for* God.

In the first place, being present for God involves what the twentieth-century Anglican theologian John Macquarrie calls "letting God be." In the second, being present for God requires us to become what the apostle Paul called "ambassadors for Christ." Let's examine each in turn.

In ordinary speech, expressions like "Let me be!" or "Let her be!" have a rather passive connotation, suggesting inactivity rather than activity. "Letting-be" in this sense implies a hands-off restraint from interfering with another's business. We allow her to go about her affairs, or we insist she do the same for us. The accent is on the verb "to let," which here means to refrain from mucking about in another's life, thereby giving her room to do whatever she wishes.

But when it comes to letting God be, the connotation is more active than passive. Moreover, the accent is on the verb "to be." Letting God be means that we recognize (are present to) his mysteriously incomprehensible nature, and that we respect, embrace, and celebrate the darkness he is without trying to force him into the confinements of thinghood.[25]

Thinging God, just like thinging ourselves or other persons, is of course convenient for us. It absolves us from the frequently burdensome necessity of caring, since we needn't worry about the well-being of objects. They're disposable, remember? But we've already seen the violence we do when we accept ourselves as "me" things or crowd and teacup others into "its." The damage arises from the fact that we refuse to let ourselves or others be what we and they really are. Self-discovery and spiritual progress are thereby retarded. Something analogous may be said to take place when we refuse to let God be the no-thinged Presence he is. In shoving him into our comfortably pietistic categories, we do damage to God (as well as, obviously, to ourselves). We block the channels along which the grace-gifts of meaning, intimacy, and creativity flow. This refusal to gratefully accept God for who he is cannot but wound him. When we refuse to let God *be,* we become willing accomplices in his daily murder atop Golgotha. Our lack of caring is the crucifix on which he hangs.

But when we make ourselves caringly present for God, we actively invite him to come forth as the darkly brilliant *Khora* he is. This invitation, in fact, is affirmation: affirmation of his unknowability, affirmation of his no-thingness, affirmation of his impenetrable mystery. It's also celebration: celebration of the fact that divine Presence, perplexing, awesome, and at times even terrifying, is precisely what bestows meaning and intimacy and creativity upon ourselves, others, and, indeed, all of reality as well. Letting God be is invitation, affirmation, and celebration, and all three have as their one and only goal the well-being of Presence.

This doesn't mean that we won't occasionally long for the user-friendly god-things we worship in our atheistic lapses. We may sometimes feel a twinge of nostalgia for the days when God was an uncomplicated and readily accessible object to be pulled out at our convenience. But we willingly live without such cheap consolations for the sake of God's well-being. In being present for God, we care too much for him to deny his *Khora*-nature, and we gladly sacrifice our old complacency in order to give him the only gift we can: the freedom to be what he is. We endure those occasional dark nights when God's Absence outweighs God's Presence, just as we face with courage the fact that even our experiences of divine Presence is always (at least in this life) filtered through the cloud of unknowing. And we do all this not for our own sakes but for his, so that he, the Supreme Is-Who-Is-Not, might *be*. As the contemporary Trappist Dom Stephen puts it, "We simply have to allow God to be. That's what it really is all about, isn't it? Not easy for adults who have been taught to imprint themselves on as much of life as they can."[26]

Being caringly present for God doesn't stop here. If God's well-being is served when we as individuals let him be, it only stands to reason that his well-being is progressively enhanced when others do the same. So the person who genuinely cares for God can't rest content with just privately presencing for God. She longs to encourage others to likewise invite, affirm, and celebrate the divine Presence—first for God's good, then for theirs. To that end, she joyfully accepts what St. Paul calls "the ministry of reconciliation":

> God . . . through Christ reconciled us to himself and gave us the ministry of reconciliation; that is, in Christ God was reconciling the world to himself, not counting their trespasses against them, and entrusting to us the message of reconciliation. So we are ambassadors for Christ, God making his appeal through us (2 Corinthians 5:18–20).

Paul's use of the word "ambassador" is particularly revealing. The Greek is *presbeutes*.

It's a legal and political term that had two interrelated meanings in the ancient world. The first implied that a *presbeutes* was someone with a direct commission from whomever she served. The second suggested that a *presbeutes* was responsible for bringing others into the service of her master. These two meanings spell out the poles of Paul's "ministry of reconciliation." The person who has attuned to *Khora* and thereby herself has become "almost divine," as the *Cloud*'s author puts it, receives a commission from God to become his agent on earth. Just as she has been brought into the fullness of being by divine grace, so she is now entrusted, as we saw in the previous chapter, with extending the domain of being by nurturing others. She becomes Simeon's sword and, in ministering to her sisters and brothers by opening their hearts to God, also helps consolidate the ruptured Body of Christ. Her care for God's well-being necessarily bleeds over into care for her fellow Christs. And in effecting their reconciliation with *Khora,* she both enhances the community of human presences in which her own identity is situated and lets God be the all-encompassing Presence he is.

The universe is threaded through with the web of caring. Touch one string, and the whole is connaturally affected. Care for God necessarily encompasses the self and others. Care for self and others necessarily points to care for God. When creatures have shed their alienated thinghood and dwell in the great clearing of divine Presence; when the heart of every person—and the mysterious heart of the entire universe as well—has split open to reveal the saving words of the *dialogismoi kardion;* when the dark *Khora* of divine Presence has called forth the deep-down spiritual nobility—the holiness—within each and every human being, and reconciled us to our final destiny as saints: then the *parousia* of the endtime will truly have come. The promised morning star will rise in the heavens, and all that it shines upon will be Presence.

Chopping Wood, Drawing Water

I began this book with the suggestion that the proper goal of human existence is sainthood, a steady growth into the God-like holiness that is our destiny. Yet we frequently stymie our spiritual progression by demanding too much of ourselves. We fancy that the only way to be holy is to love as God loves, to radiate the same loving-kindness that Scripture assures us is the most essential characteristic of God. Anything less than this, we believe, falls woefully short of the mark. So we often rush headlong toward the finish line without taking the time to prepare ourselves for the race. It's little wonder that many of us become so winded after a very short while that we find it impossible to stay the course.

The goal of loving as God loves is admirable, but the impetuosity with which we tend to dash toward it is foolish. There simply is no fast track when it comes to holiness, and to ignore this bespeaks a certain degree of impatient arrogance rather than humble longing. Most of us aren't even sure what it means to love well and truly at the human level, much less at the divine. Yet we convince ourselves that if we but struggle mightily to make heroic efforts we will get where we wish to go. It takes only a few years of sad experience to discover the folly of this assumption. When that dismal truth dawns on us, we needlessly fall into frustration, self-contempt, and despair. We may even become so demoralized that we wash our hands of the whole affair and cynically dismiss love as just another "four-letter word."

Given these risks, perhaps it would be well to do the same thing with the word *love* that Eckhart and Tillich recommend for the word *God:* if it proves a stumbling block, throw it out until such time as we're able to better appreciate what it means. Confess one's confusion, honestly appraise the

laxness of one's spiritual muscles, and submit to a prelimi-
nary regimen. Forgo, even if only temporarily, the high road
of love, and concentrate on the more modest path of caring.
Realize that at least for the moment this "little way" is better
suited for us than the flashier goal of full-fledged love. Walk
before we try to run. Chop wood and draw water, as the Zen
disciple we met in the Introduction was instructed to do. Concentrate single-mindedly on the apparently mundane and
frequently burdensome chores at hand, and let the ultimate
goal of "enlightenment" take care of itself.

If we pursue the little way of caring with resolve and
humility, the same wondrous thing that happened to the disciple befalls us. As our hands callous and our muscles tighten,
we grow, almost imperceptibly, into the holiness ordained for
us. We become ever more aware of the spiritually noble self
that defines our true identity and, in the process, begin to
notice the spiritual nobility of others as well. We drop our
frightened and alienated habits of thinging both ourselves and
our fellows and, instead, open up in care to the sacred presences we and they are. And as we become progressively present
to and for the holiness that connaturally links us with them,
we find ourselves slowly but surely entering into a deeply caring heart-relationship with the Presence who graciously cared
us into existence in the first place, and who continues to
enfold us in an embrace that is darkly but profoundly meaningful, inexpressibly but wonderfully intimate, unfathomably
but unmistakably creative. Care leads to *cor; cor* nudges us
toward *kara; kara* leads us to *Khora.*

The upshot of this cumulative, sometimes scarcely per-
ceptible growth into presence is that we, like the Zen disciple,
awaken one day to discover that we *are.* The *rhomphaia* that
so silently went about its work in our hardened hearts fin-
ishes the task, and we come into the full existence intended

for us from the very beginning. We become human. We cross the finish line to arrive at sainthood—and all because we trustingly persevered in the tasks of chopping wood and drawing water.

Then the greatest mystery of all unconceals, for we discover that the regimen of caring to which we submitted has somehow brought us to a new state of being: one in which we open completely to self, others, and God, and long with all our heart, soul, and mind to cooperate in the grand task of coaxing all creation into wholeness. Conventional labels and ordinary words can't possibly come close to capturing the wondrous richness of this moment. They seem, in fact, quite beside the point. Why bother with them? But if we had to choose a single word by which to awkwardly gesture at this newfound fullness of being, what better one could we select than *love*?

In liberating us from our hardened hearts and opening us up to presence, the sword/Word gives us what we always had: the divine Heart. As God told Catherine of Siena in the fourteenth century, "See, dearest daughter, a few days ago I took your heart from you; now, in the same way, I give you my own heart."[27] In our own time, Henri Nouwen puts the matter more directly when he writes that the heart "is the place where all is one in God, the place where we truly belong, the place from which we come and to which we always yearn to return."[28]

And that place is Love.

This is what Simeon saw so many centuries ago when he stood in the temple portico and gazed upon the Presence he held in his arms, the Presence that still indwells our hearts today.

ENDNOTES

Introduction: BECOMING SAINTS

The epigraph from Irenaeus is cited in George A. Maloney, *Gold, Frankincense, and Myrrh: An Introduction to Eastern Christian Spirituality* (New York: Crossroad, 1997), p. 17.

1. Graham Greene, *The Power and the Glory* (New York: Penguin, 1982), p. 210.

2. Augustine, *Confessions*, trans. Henry Chadwick (New York: Oxford University Press, 1992), Book VIII, p. 145.

3. Thomas Merton, *Life and Holiness* (New York: Doubleday, 1996), p. 24.

4. Thomas Merton, *Entering the Silence*, ed. Jonathan Montaldo. *The Diaries of Thomas Merton*, Volume 2 (San Francisco: Harper, 1997), p. 451.

5. Simone Weil, *Waiting for God*, trans. Emma Craufurd (New York: Harper & Row, 1971), p. 149.

6. C. S. Lewis, "The Weight of Glory," in *The Weight of Glory and Other Addresses* (New York: Collier, 1980), p. 19.

7. Dietrich Bonhoeffer, *Letters and Papers from Prison,* trans. Reginald H. Fuller (New York: Macmillan, 1966), p. 175.

8. C. A. Anderson Scott, *New Testament Ethics* (New York: Macmillan, 1930), p. 23.

9. Thérèse of Lisieux, *Story of a Soul,* trans. John Clarke, O.C.S. (Washington, DC: ICS Publications, 1996), p. 209.

10. T. S. Eliot, "Ash Wednesday," in *Collected Poems, 1909–1962* (New York: Harcourt, Brace & World, 1971), p. 67.

1. SIMEON'S RIDDLE

The chapter epigraph is from Gerald Vann, *The Divine Pity* (London: Fontana, 1985), pp. 26–27.

1. Raymond E. Brown provides a good summary of Patristic interpretations of Simeon's oracle in his magisterial *The Birth of the Messiah* (New York: Doubleday, 1993), pp. 460–466.

2. Popular devotion to the seven sorrows of Mary was institutionalized in the early thirteenth century with the establishment of the Order of Friar Servants of Mary, or the Servites. The dolorous swords that pierce her heart are, traditionally, Simeon's prophecy (Luke 2:34–35); the flight into Egypt and the massacre of the Innocents (Matthew 2:13–18); losing the Holy Child in Jerusalem (Luke 2:41–51); meeting Jesus on his way to Golgotha (Luke 23:27–18); standing at the foot of the cross (John 19:25–27); Jesus being taken from the cross (Luke 23:50–53); and the burial of Jesus (Luke 23:55–56).

3. Quoted in Anthony Bloom, *Beginning to Pray* (New York: Paulist Press, 1970), p. 19.

4. John Donne, "Ecologue 1613. December 26," in *The Complete English Poems,* ed. A. J. Smith (New York: Penguin, 1981), p. 140.

5. *The Desert Fathers*, ed. and trans. Helen Waddell (New York: Vintage, 1998), p. 71.

6. Karl Barth, *Christmas*, trans. Bernhard Citron (Edinburgh: Oliver & Boyd, 1959), p. 56.

7. George Herbert, "Jesu," in *The English Poems of George Herbert*, ed. C. A. Patrides (London: Dent, 1984), p. 125.

8. William Cowper, "The Task," in *Poetical Works* (New York: Dutton, 1894), pp. 98–99.

9. Thomas Merton, *Conjectures of a Guilty Bystander* (New York: Doubleday, 1989), p. 18.

10. Jean-Paul Sartre, *No Exit*, trans. Stuart Gilbert (New York: Vintage, 1949).

11. Paul Tillich, *Systematic Theology* (Chicago: University of Chicago Press, 1953), Volume 1, p. 49.

12. Rudolf Otto, *The Idea of the Holy*, trans. John W. Harvey (London: Oxford University Press, 1950).

13. Thomas Aquinas, *Summa Theologica*, I, 1, 6, ad 3; II, II, 45, 2.

2. CARING FOR SELF

The chapter epigraph is from Thomas Traherne, "My Spirit," in *Centuries, Poems, and Thanksgivings,* ed. H. M. Margoliouth (Oxford: The Clarendon Press, 1958), Volume 2, p. 56.

1. David Hume, *A Treatise on Human Nature,* ed. D. G. C. Macnabb (London: Fontana, 1975), Book I, pp. 300–302.

2. Fyodor Dostoevsky, *Notes from Underground*, trans. Michael R. Katz (New York: W. W. Norton, 1989), p. 5.

3. Ibid., p. 1.

4. Ibid., p. 4.

5. Ibid.

6. Ibid., pp. 9–10.

7. Ibid., pp. 7, 10.

8. Henry David Thoreau, *Walden*, in *The Portable Thoreau*, ed. Carl Bode (New York: Viking, 1974), p. 263.

9. Karl Rahner, "The Experience of God Today," in *Theological Investigations XI*, trans. David Bourke (New York: Seabury Press, 1974), p. 159.

10. Meister Eckhart, Sermon 1, in *Meister Eckhart: A Modern Translation*, trans. and ed. Raymond Bernard Blakney (New York: Harper & Row, 1941), pp. 99, 100. Eckhart also discusses spiritual nobility in his treatise "The Aristocrat," pp. 74–81.

11. Ibid., p. 99.

12. Martin Heidegger, "The End of Philosophy and the Task of Thinking," in *Basic Writings*, ed. David Farrell Krell (San Francisco: Harper, 1993), p. 441.

13. Meister Eckhart, Sermon 1, p. 97.

14. Maximos the Confessor, "Various Texts on Theology, the Divine Economy, and Virtue and Vice," in *The Philokalia*, trans. and ed. G. E. H. Palmer, Philip Sherrard, Kallistos Ware (London: Faber & Faber, 1981), Volume 2, p. 45.

15. Meister Eckhart, Sermon 12, p. 153.

16. Ibid.

17. Ibid., Sermon 24, pp. 210–211.

18. Ibid., Sermon 5, p. 125.

19. Martin Heidegger, "Building Dwelling Thinking," in *Basic Writings*, p. 363.

20. Meister Eckhart, Sermon 19, p. 184.

21. Quoted by Meister Eckhart, Sermon 1, p. 101.

22. Ibid., Sermon 2, p. 105.

23. Ibid., Sermon 1, pp. 99, 104.

24. Ibid, p. 104.

25. Paul Tillich, *The Courage to Be* (London: Fontana, 1974).

26. Josef Pieper, *About Love*, trans. Richard and Clara Winston, in *Faith, Hope, Love* (San Francisco: Ignatius Press, 1997), p. 194.

3. CARING FOR OTHERS

The chapter epigraph is from *The Notebooks of Simone Weil,* trans. Arthur Wills (London: Routledge & Kegan Paul, 1976), Volume 1, p. 239.

1. Kurt Vonnegut, *God Bless You, Mr. Rosewater* (New York: Dell, 1978), pp. 43, 42.

2. Ibid., p. 42.

3. Ibid., p. 43.

4. Thomas Merton, "The Time of the End Is the Time of No Room," in *A Thomas Merton Reader,* ed. Thomas P. McDonnell (New York: Doubleday, 1996), p. 361.

5. Ibid., p. 363.

6. Ibid., pp. 363, 364.

7. Henri Nouwen, *Intimacy: Essays in Pastoral Psychology* (San Francisco: Harper, 1981), p. 24.

8. Ibid., p. 25.

9. Kurt Vonnegut, *God Bless You, Mr. Rosewater,* p. 43.

10. Robert J. Wicks and Thomas E. Rodgerson, *Companions in Hope: The Art of Christian Caring* (New York: Paulist, 1998), pp. 183–184.

11. Thomas Merton, *Conjectures of a Guilty Bystander* (New York: Doubleday, 1989), pp. 156, 157.

12. Ibid., p. 158.

13. Ibid., p. 157.

14. Søren Kierkegaard, *Practice in Christianity*, trans. Howard V. and Edna H. Hong (Princeton: Princeton University Press, 1991), p. 63.

15. Ibid.

16. Ibid., p. 64.

17. Thomas Merton, *Entering the Silence*, ed. Jonathan Montaldo. *The Journals of Thomas Merton,* Volume 2 (San Francisco: Harper, 1997), p. 265.

18. Thomas Merton, *Conjectures of a Guilty Bystander,* p. 157.

19. Ibid., p. 158.

20. Ibid.

21. Simone Weil, *Waiting for God*, trans. Emma Craufurd (New York: Harper & Row, 1973), p. 149.

22. Ibid., p. 144.

23. Ibid., pp. 144, 147, 146.

24. Ibid., pp. 145, 147.

25. Ibid., p. 148.

26. Ibid., p. 147.

27. Ibid., p. 150.

28. Ibid.

29. Ibid., p. 151.

4. CARING FOR GOD

The chapter epigraph is from Dionysius the Areopagite, *The Divine Names and Mystical Theology,* trans. John D. Jones (Milwaukee: Marquette University Press, 1980), p. 175. I've slightly rearranged the passage's syntax but left its meaning intact.

1. Meister Eckhart, Sermon 28, in *Meister Eckhart: A Modern Translation*, trans. and ed. Raymond B. Blakney (New York: Harper & Row, 1941), p. 231.

2. Paul Tillich, "The Depth of Existence," in *The Shaking of the Foundations* (New York: Charles Scribner's Sons, 1948), p. 57.

3. Plato, *Timaeus*, trans. Benjamin Jowett, in *Collected Dialogues*, ed. Edith Hamilton and Huntington Cairns (Princeton: Princeton University Press, 1973), 49a–51c. The contemporary French philosopher Jacques Derrida is also fascinated with the notion of God as *Khora*. Two essays in particular are important (and, unusual for Derrida, accessible!): "*Khora*," in *On the Name*, trans. David Wood, John P. Leavey, Jr., and Ian McLeod (Stanford, CA: Stanford University Press, 1995), pp. 89–127; and "How to Avoid Speaking: Denials," in *Derrida and Negative Theology*, ed. Harold Coward and Toby Foshay (Albany: State University of New York Press, 1992), pp. 73–142.

4. Graham Greene, *The Power and the Glory* (New York: Penguin, 1982), p. 169.

5. For a more detailed discussion of the various ways in which we thing God, interested readers may wish to consult my *Soul Wilderness: A Desert Spirituality* (New York: Paulist, 2001).

6. Thomas Aquinas, *Faith, Reason, and Theology: Questions I–IV of his Commentary on the De Trinitate of Boethius*, trans. Armand Maurer (Toronto: Pontifical Institute of Medieval Studies, 1987), Q. 1, Article 2.

7. Thomas Aquinas, *Quaestiones Disputatae*, quoted in Josef Pieper, *The Silence of St. Thomas*, trans. John Murray, S.J., and Daniel O'Connor (Chicago: Henry Regnery, 1965), p. 69.

8. Simone Weil, *The Notebooks of Simone Weil*, trans. Arthur Wills (London: Routledge & Kegan Paul, 1976), Volume 1, p. 240; *Gravity and Grace*, trans. Arthur Wills (New York: G. P. Putnam's Sons, 1952), p. 86.

9. Dionysius the Areopagite, *The Divine Names and Mystical Theology*, p. 225.

10. Ibid., p. 211.

11. Ibid., p. 214.

12. Ibid., p. 222.

13. Ibid., p. 226.

14. *The Cloud of Unknowing,* ed. William Johnston (New York: Doubleday, 1973), p. 84.

15. Ibid., p. 49.

16. Ibid., p. 53.

17. Ibid., p. 83.

18. Ibid., p. 54.

19. Ibid.

20. Ibid., p. 55.

21. Ibid., p. 136.

22. Ibid., pp. 80, 98.

23. Ibid., p. 95.

24. Ibid., p. 135.

25. Macquarrie discusses letting God be in many of his works. See, for example, *In Search of Humanity: A Theological and Philosophical Approach* (New York: Crossroad, 1983), pp. 180–181, and his magisterial *Principles of Christian Theology* (New York: Charles Scribner's Sons, 1977), pp. 113–119, 200–230, 348–350.

26. Quoted in Frank Bianco, *Voices of Silence: Lives of the Trappists Today* (New York: Doubleday, 1992), p. 201.

27. From Raymond of Capua's *Life of Catherine of Siena,* quoted in Suzanne Noffke, O.P., *Catherine of Siena: Vision through a Distant Eye* (Collegeville, MN: Liturgical Press, 1996), p. 32.

28. Henri Nouwen, *The Road to Daybreak: A Spiritual Journey* (New York: Doubleday, 1988), p. 49.